LONDON
Sight Unseen

To my nephew Tom

LONDON
Sight Unseen

BY SNOWDON

TEXT BY GWYN HEADLEY

WEIDENFELD & NICOLSON

Foreword

ALTHOUGH half Welsh I was born at Eaton Terrace in 1930. I have lived all my adult life in London. When I was five I was sent to a girls' school called Frances Holland with my sister which was just round the corner. Perhaps unsurprisingly it is still vivid in my mind – I think I am their only 'Old Boy'. My father had a restless spirit and so we were constantly on the move. Seventeen homes came and went in as many years, from a huge terraced house in Chelsea to a garret in Charing Cross Road. We never knew where we were, or where we would be next, let alone where our toys might be. Perhaps that has made me particularly attached to my house in Kensington where I have remained long enough to see the trees grow tall and for the ivy to cover as much of the view as my neighbours will tolerate.

I have always had a taste for the secret garden and the individual house. My first London nest was certainly the smallest and most secret – a minute box room over the Porter's Lodge in Albany, Piccadilly off the chambers my father had taken, now deemed too small for habitation. The window was a Georgian fanlight that seemed to grow out of the floor.

My maternal great grandfather, Linley Sambourne, a *Punch* cartoonist and pioneer photographer, lived in what I thought as a child was the gloomiest possible Victorian pile in Stafford Terrace behind Kensington High Street. Luckily it is now much more appreciated by the Victorian Society to which my mother gave it in an especially enlightened moment. But architecture was in her blood, and her uncle Alfred Messel's buildings in Berlin were avant-garde structures of glass and steel at the end of the nineteenth century, all sadly flattened in the War. It was her brother, my uncle, Oliver Messel the theatre designer, who taught me to use my eyes. He inspired me to love architectural detail, literally to look up to it. One of life's greatest pleasures was walking with him through Venice at night peering at every cornice and architrave.

At Cambridge, I naturally studied architecture but perhaps rather too much from my seat as a cox for the Cambridge eight, looking at buildings on the river bank instead of where we were going. Luckily we won anyway. But I failed my exams because I had not finished my portfolio. I did, however, complete a thesis on the River Thames and its importance to London. I proposed lock-gates below Tower Bridge to

John Betjeman wrote a description of life in my room beneath the bay window at 59 Rotherhithe Street in an article for the *Daily Telegraph*. The house and the entire street were demolished by Bermondsey Council and replaced by a concrete walkway in the early 1960s.

make the whole river non-tidal like the Seine and to make it easily navigable for fast river buses. In those days St Paul's still had its proper relationship to the river, subsequently hidden by appalling structures of the 1960s and '70s.

I also proposed to redevelop the south side for all income groups, to prevent the river being a social barrier, which it certainly was then and still is to a certain degree. A city works for me only when you have people from every walk of life and of every kind, living cheek by jowl. In some new developments like Chelsea Harbour, shops selling the nuts and bolts of life are nowhere to be found. I do not like a city where the rich hog their penthouse loft developments all along the river while the less fortunate are hidden behind their net curtains at the rear.

It was because I failed my architecture exams that I started taking photographs. With my Uncle Oliver's encouragement I began taking pictures for the theatre. In 1957 my first book was published, by George Weidenfeld. It was called simply, *London*, but it was really about the people. Londoners, more than architecture. I had rented a small room in Rotherhithe, which I converted from a coal store into a glorious bed-sit. I did the washing-up at high tide when the water came up to the window and at low tide climbed down a chain and walked along the beach to the pub. The whole point of being on the river is to be as near to it as possible rather than stuck up in a high-rise block with a 'wonderful view' of the river.

The sounds of the river were as important as the sight of it, and my friends loved the room as much as I did. To name drop for a moment, I remember especially an evening with Noel Coward and Marlene Dietrich at the piano singing far into the night. Idiotically I had no camera, nor tape recorder for that matter, but perhaps the memory is all the more extraordinary for that reason.

In about 1960 John Betjeman's house in Cloth Fair burnt down (ironically as it had survived the great fire of London in 1666) and I lent my room to him. He rewarded me with this description of being there in the *Daily Telegraph*:

...my bedroom hung over the Thames, with a tremendous view. Up-stream I could see the dome of St Paul's framed in the silhouette of Tower Bridge. Down-stream I looked towards the masts, funnels and cranes in the Pool of London. On the opposite bank were the wharves and Georgian brick buildings of Wapping.

'The air was always fresh and with a hint of the sea in it. At night, with the lights reflecting in the water, the scene was equally enthralling. Passing craft were a continual interest. I put my bed on the river side of the room and it was delicious to go to sleep to the solacing sounds of water.

'At low tide there would be the distant chug of a passing tug and a few seconds later the swish of the waves caused by her wake rippling over the pebbles and mud below my window. At high tide after a tug had passed the water made a plopping sound right against my bedroom wall as though I were in a ship's hold.

It was the most restful few months I had ever spent in London. The people of Rotherhithe were a friendly village with a life of their own. Taking a ticket to London from that obscure Underground station at the southern opening of Sir Marc Brunel's Thames Tunnel was like setting off from home into a stranger land...

Despite his and my campaign to save the street, it was demolished by order of Bermondsey local council. All that remains is a windy concrete walkway, apart from the solitary coal merchants on page 75.

I love silly architectural jokes. I love kitsch and quite frequently I hate 'good taste' when it is a kind of pretentious uniform for people who do not know what else to wear. I am not against the modern in any sense of the word, only the mediocre. When I designed the aviary at London Zoo with Frank Newby and Cedric Price in 1963, we wanted to push the boundaries of structure to their limits. In a way it is a folly because it fools the eye, appearing to float on its two points of compression with the ground. We were extremely flattered when it was listed last year. I like the sense of drama and surprise in architecture which is often a matter of scale and contrast. I prefer high camp to solid classicism and the bastardised 'Palladianism' or 'repro Jaco' of the London rich.

Kenneth Clark said of Leonardo that he was an 'inquisitive man'. I cannot think of a greater compliment. In humble emulation of Leonardo I hope this is an inquisitive book that might prove to be infectious. I want people to be surprised that these places are in London at all...

The illustrations do not pretend to be great architectural photographs; mainly they are glimpses, photographs taken when I was on my way from one place to another. Sometimes I would find that an old architectural friend had gone or was changed forever, others like the prefab houses (page 18) that were erected supposedly for a few years' life after the war, have become admirable survivors, all the more delightful when they keep grand company. The one on page 18 is bang next door to the Archbishop of Canterbury's Palace at Lambeth.

It is above all the hidden secrets of London that I love and which I have gathered together here for fun. Much credit must go to Gwyn Headley who showed and guided me round many of the places I didn't know myself. It is for all of us that relish the surprise of going down narrow passages that open on to unknown hidden vistas. Perhaps you will know many of them. I am certain you will discover more, such is London's architectural richness and unique character.

Snowdon
London, 1999

Pictures

Grotto, Hampton Court House, Hampton

Upon a certain Grotto near Hampton
by A Tenant of the Manor
A Grotto this, by Mortal Hand!
O no – we tread in fairy Land
'Tis raised by Mab's enchanted Wand,
So rare, so elegant, so bright,
It dazzles, while it charms the sight.

Hampton Court House was built in 1757 by the 2nd Earl of Halifax, George Montagu Dunk (he added the euphonious 'Dunk' in order to benefit from an advantageous marriage settlement) on eight acres of public land which he simply appropriated. As he was Ranger of Bushey Park and a favourite of the King, he was able to do much as he pleased. The house was built for his mistress, Mrs Anna Maria Donaldson, a singer employed by Halifax as 'governess' for his children. As the poem above was published on 22 July 1769, it is probable that it was written to mark the completion of the grotto – the 'Tenant of the Manor' was the great actor-manager David Garrick.

Among the later tenants of Hampton Court House was the 4th Earl of Sandwich, who lived here between 1775 and 1780. He was so loathe to leave the gaming table that he ordered his beef to be brought to him between two slices of bread, an aristocratic contribution to the fast food industry. The Grotto was prominently marked on a 1903 estate map prepared for the sale of the house, which sat unsold on the market for nine years. It became an old ladies' home after the war, run by Middlesex County Council, and the grotto was restored to its present shell-encrusted glory by Diana Reynell and Belinda Eade in 1986.

Gipsy caravan, South London
Whether this was on its way to a rally of gipsy caravan owners in Morden or a genuine hangover from romantic Romany days is not known, but the horse was an authentic gipsy piebald, with a very long mane.

Gipsy carriages, Culvert Place, Battersea
These gipsy caravans still have their wheels boarded up underneath. The gipsies had this spandrel-shaped plot of land between two railway lines in Battersea until after the war, when they were moved to a purpose-built site at Swanley in Kent. The carriages are still lived in and remain on their sordid, rattling little site, hemmed in by tracks, stonemasons and garages.

Porter's Lodge, Chelsea Studios, Fulham Road
There is something Gallic about this tiny lodge – and the unstudied nonchalance of the bicycle.

Cricket Scoreboard, Grove Park, Chiswick
A tiny tall temple of simple Palladian elegance to some obscure rite, standing alone on open parkland like an eye-catcher from some forgotten mansion, proves on inspection to be just that; this is the scoreboard for the University of Westminster's cricket pitch at Chiswick, built on what was formerly the Duke of Devonshire's estate at Grove Park.
    ERECTED IN MEMORY OF GEORGE OGILVIE ('PA')
    FOUNDER MEMBER AND OFFICIAL OF THE POLYTECHNIC
    CRICKET CLUB
    1875 TO 1947
    BY HIS FELLOW MEMBERS
    1949

Gardener's Hut, Lincoln's Inn

Queen Victoria paid a visit to the legal enclave of Lincoln's Inn in 1852, and the benchers laid out £860 for 'extra fittings' for the event, along with £3,988 for the grounds and gardens. Buried somewhere in those sums must be the expense of building 'at a Cost not to exceed £150' this tiny temple for Mr Temple the gardener. By a strange coincidence the plaque above the south side bears the arms of Christopher Temple, the Treasurer of Lincoln's Inn for the same year. Philip Hardwick, who designed the demolished Euston Arch, was the architect to the Society at the time, but the actual author is most likely to have been George Wigg, the long-serving Surveyor to the Benchers, reinterpreting Hardwick's designs for the Stone Buildings behind this temple. In 1998 the hut was restored and the concrete tiled roof was replaced with the more appropriate lead. Inside, instead of the usual old rope, decaying hosepipes and holed buckets such buildings accrue, is a chair and a small desk with a selection of gardening books.

Porter's Lodge, Natural History Museum, South Kensington, *right*

'I shall want space for seventy whales, to begin with,' demanded Richard Owen, the first curator of the Natural History Museum. After an unenthusiastic beginning – a member of the Athenaeum complained that 'out of the 50 trustees of the British Museum [of which the Natural History Museum was a division] not more than three or four have shown any symptoms of interest in natural history' – Victorian drive and energy was in due course fully committed to this powerful, massive museum designed by the industrious Alfred Waterhouse. His Town Hall at Manchester is held to be his masterpiece, but this lodge, a miniature of the Natural History Museum, shows his attention to the smallest details, a perfect foil to the claymore of the main building.

The museum was begun in 1873 and opened in 1881 at a cost of £350,000 'without any ceremony beyond that of setting the doors apart', noted *The Times*, which went on to allow that the new museum was 'almost as great an advance on the Museum at Bloomsbury as that was on the old curiosity shops of still earlier days'.

Clarence House Lodge, The Mall, *above*

This is a very small house indeed, thankful to be adopted by Clarence House after it lost its *raison d'être* as the park keeper's lodge when the Mall was driven through St James's Park to allow ceremonial processions. As a result it has the singular distinction of being the only house on the Mall. Like many other lodges it can boast a distinguished architect: in this case Sir Robert Smirke, designer of the British Museum, who built it in 1838 at a cost of £730. In the 1960s it was home to the then well-known Birdman of St James.

Wellington Barracks, Birdcage Walk, Westminster, *right*

The monumentality of the barracks stands in heavy opposition to the airiness of the street they face. The prettily named Birdcage Walk was purely descriptive: Charles II had cages of songbirds hanging from every tree along the avenue. The barracks were built in 1833 by an engineer, advised by Philip Hardwick whose assured touch with Doric is clearly seen. The barracks have had more than their share of misfortune – during repairs in 1856 a cornice collapsed, killing a workman, and in 1890 Elizabeth and Fanny Ackersgill, the young daughters of an officer at the barracks, were burnt to death in a fire. The greatest tragedy was the bombing of the Guards Chapel in 1944 when over 100 worshippers were killed. The guardsman on the railings has been a victim of defence cuts, and is no longer at his post.

Uni-Seco Prefab, Royal Street, London

In May 1944 five designs for pre-fabricated houses – 'prefabs' – were shown at the Tate Gallery in answer to the Temporary Housing Act of that year, an attempt to solve the looming post-war housing crisis. Building started in 1945 and over the next four years 160,000 prefabs were scattered across Britain. Designed to last ten years at the most, people are still happily living in them over fifty years later, which is either an indictment of or credit to planners, depending on your point of view. Enthusiatic prefab spotters will immediately identify this as a Uni-Seco, the commonest species in London. This was built by the Universal Selection Engineering Co., based in south London, and identifying marks include the rather daring corner window frame on the right, the glassfibre porch and the flat roof. Over 30,000 were built, and only now are they finally beginning to disappear from our streets, not without regret – an assembly of prefabs in Birmingham has been listed as a conservation area by English Heritage.

Segal Houses, Walters Way, Lewisham

The Austrian architect Walter Segal was one of many to promote the benefits of low-cost, functional, owner-builder houses, but unlike most he made his dream work. The first Segal house was designed and erected out of necessity: in 1962 Segal was moving house, and, needing temporary accommodation, he sketched out an idea and built it in a Highgate garden, where it remains today. This little locality of crisp minimalist Segal houses stands in a cul-de-sac named after their creator, the only architect to have two London roads named after him during his lifetime.

Collins Square, Blackheath

Collins Square is an alleyway off Tranquil Vale, which manages to squeeze in these charmingly Kentish rustic black clapboarded cottages, the closest vernacular builders got to pre-fabs. They were built in 1798 by a developer named John Collins as a village within a village. By the 1950s the row was looking woebegone, and in 1961 the council issued a demolition order. The Blackheath Society stirred up popular opinion and saved the cottages, which were restored by the architect Neil Macfadyen in 1964.

Shell Pavilions, Grosvenor Gardens, Victoria

This pretty little shell-encrusted pavilion stands in a little triangle of land by Victoria station known as Lower Grosvenor Gardens after the Duke of Westminster gave it to the City of Westminster. The statue of Marshal Foch in the small garden was unveiled by the Prince of Wales, later the Duke of Windsor, in 1930, and the two shell pavilions were the gift of the French government, but well after the Second World War. The architect-in-chief of the National Monuments and Palaces of France, M. Jean Moreux, laid out the tiny park with its gravel arabesque walks and a brightly coloured floral fleur-de-lis centrepiece. The garden was dedicated to the memory of the Marshal by M. Massigli, the French Ambassador, in 1952. The shell pavilions, one for the attendant and one for the garden tools, were designed by M. Moreux in the manner of eighteenth-century French *fabriques*, or follies, and coated with sea shells bought from France, although the *Sphere* commented rather ungraciously that 'some suitable shells were sent over from France but it is to be expected the majority will be found on British beaches.'

Toll Booth, Albert Bridge, Chelsea

Albert Bridge, the most elegant and fanciful of all London's bridges, was started in 1864 then abandoned for six years while the Government dithered about the route the Thames Embankment would take. It was finally opened in 1873. The architect Rowland Mason Ordish designed it as a rigid suspension bridge to his own patent design, but it had to be strengthened by Sir Joseph Bazalgette in 1884 when he was building the Embankment. After the Second World War the London County Council wanted to pull it down but the whole of Chelsea, led by John Betjeman protested vigorously, and it was reprieved. The bridge remains as fragile as it looks; it is open only to light traffic, and notices still famously demand that all troops must break step when marching over it. Four tollbooths were built for the Albert Bridge Company, which spent all its capital on the bridge, budgeting nothing for the muddy and rutted approach roads.

Duck Island Cottage, St James's Park, Westminster

Most aptly named, this little house was built in the middle of the capital for the now defunct Ornithological Society of London in 1840. In July of that year the Society had presented Prince Albert with a pair of ortolans, and by September the papers were reporting that 'an ornamental building in the Swiss style, consisting of council-room, bridge, and keeper's cottage, is now building in St James's-park for the Ornithological Society of London. The site is nearly opposite the Horse Guards, and the design, approved by the Board of Works, has been prepared by Mr. Watson, under whose direction it will be completed.' The cottage contained a steam-powered heating system for the incubation of eggs, and in 1857 a spring productive enough to supply the whole lake was discovered on the island. Now the London Gardens Trust is fortunate enough to have the cottage as their headquarters.

Gate Lodge, Ely Place, Holborn

Ely Place is the archetypal London street: tall, prosperous Georgian buildings, solid, trustworthy, elegant and private – so private it is gated and guarded by a beadle. His tiny one-room lodge is nothing more than a door, a window, a fireplace and a chimney. The chimney supported by the window is puzzling, but the flue turns an S-bend from the fireplace in the side wall so the chimney can be raised above the façade. This was the site of the palace of the bishops of Ely in Cambridgeshire, and therefore out of the jurisdiction of London.

Porter's Lodge, Middle Temple

'Dainty', comments Pevsner on this tiny lodge hiding behind railings on the Embankment, cowering in front of the judicial majesty of the Inner and Middle Temples. It was built in 1880, and followed the tradition of all new buildings at the Inns of Court by being inscribed with the initials of the Treasurer at the time of construction, in this case the lamb and flag signifying the Temple and 18 C T M 80.

Cowford Lodge, Buckingham Palace

Few people notice this massive yet small building, set as it is at the side of one of Britain's most popular tourist attractions. After his success with the Victoria & Albert Museum, Aston Webb became the Edwardian architect of royal choice. In 1911 he redesigned the Mall, adding Admiralty Arch at the east end and the gigantic Victoria Memorial, sculpted by Sir Thomas Brock, at the west in front of Buckingham Palace. This lodge or sentry box, whose purpose has been forgotten (it now stores spades and hoses) must have been built at that time and may well have been a police post. In 1912 Webb refaced the Palace in Portland stone quickly, competently and within budget, and was knighted as a result. As this monolith does not have a name, it might be christened Cowford Lodge. Most Londoners have forgotten that the Tyburn flows in front of Buckingham Palace, and where this structure stands was a ford over the river called Cowford.

Trinity Hospital, Greenwich
HOSPITALE
SANCTAE ET INDIVIDVAE TRINITATIS
GRENWICI
SANCTAE ET INDIVIDVAE TRINITATIS SIC GLORIA
1616

Henry Howard, Earl of Northampton, founded
Trinity Hospital, or Norfolk College, as an almshouse
in 1614, and it is still an almshouse today, run by
the Mercers' Company. Squeezed between plastic
executive houses and a 1906 power station on
the former site of Lumley Mansion, it was built to
house twelve poor men of Greenwich and eight
of Shottisham, Norfolk, where Howard had his
estate. The chapel was dedicated in 1617, and the
whole was refaced with an up-to-the-minute
white Gothick stucco façade in 1812, with a
bell-tower of which Clough Williams-Ellis, the
architect of the fantasy village of Portmeirion,
would have been proud. The building is
immaculately kept, glistening in gilt and red,
black and white.

Harbour Master's Office, Ballast Quay, Greenwich

Deep carving along the cornice proclaims this to be the Harbour Master's Office, an imposing edifice for an important man. It was built in 1854–5 by the engineer S. W. Leach at a cost of £2,200. The Thames had three harbour masters between London Bridge and Bugsby's Hole, now the site of the Millennium Dome. Each received, in addition to his salary, £5 for a servant, £2 for candles, £1 for wood, £25 for a travelling allowance and 10 tons of coal per annum.

The harbour master's role was to control collier traffic on the Thames. The post died out with the decline of river traffic, but the building remains, now converted into a grand semi-detached, near the Cutty Sark Tavern.

Isle House, Coldharbour, Old Blackwall

Contrary to popular myth, this house had nothing to do with Nelson's Lady Hamilton since it was built ten years after poor Emma died. Isle House was built at the entrance to the Blackwall Basin in 1825–6 by Sir John Rennie, architect of the Vauxhall, Southwark and Waterloo bridges over the Thames. Unromantically, it was built to house Captain Thomas Harrison, the Blackwall Dock Master for the West India Dock Company. The *London Argus* described it in 1898 as 'one of the few houses in Blackwall that can be called picturesque'.

Dock Master's House, St Katherine's Dock

Hard by Tower Bridge is St Katherine's Dock, the first part of
London's docks to be regenerated. The contractors Taylor
Woodrow bought the derelict site in the 1960s and redeveloped
it into a model of multiple-use gentrification: hotel, harbour,
pubs, restaurant, offices, residential, even a chandlery.
Unfortunately this involved the demolition of much of Philip
Hardwick's brutal industrial dock architecture, elegant in its
massive simplicity. The hapless condition of this late Georgian
gem caught the attention of Lord Snowdon, who lobbied
vigorously for its preservation, achieved with the help of Raine
Legge of the GLC. Peter Drew, the project manager for
Taylor Woodrow, made it his site office and later his home.
The 1829 house remains in private ownership, with fabulous
views down the river, as a Dock Master would need.

Cabmen's Shelters at the Natural History Museum, South Kensington; Grosvenor Gardens, Westminster; Little Venice, Bayswater; and Albert Bridge, Chelsea

Born in cold Edinburgh, the idea for these shelters was refined by the city of Birmingham where a demountable wooden shelter was produced in 1872. At the time cabmen sat outide their cabs in all weathers, so it is easy to see the attraction of the shelters, although the strictures on card-playing, alcohol and posting union notices were less popular.

The Cabmen's Shelter Fund was set up in 1875 by Sir George Armstrong, the proprietor of the *Globe* newspaper, 'for the purpose of supplying Cabmen ... with a place of shelter where they can obtain good and wholesome refreshments at very moderate prices.' Papers and even books were also supplied. The Metropolitan Police decreed that the shelters, which were built on the public highway, should not take up more space than a horse and cab. By 1889 40 shelters had been erected at a cost of about £200 each. In 1894 the fund secretary reported disapprovingly that hansom cab drivers at shelters in the smarter areas were 'extremely particular about their steaks, and their new potatoes, and their salads, and everything of that kind. They are quite as ready to complain as members of West End clubs if things are not right.'

Black Rod's Steps,
House of Lords, Westminster

When Charles Barry was rebuilding the Houses of Parliament, properly known as the Palace of Westminster (it remains officially a royal palace, even though the monarch is formally forbidden access to parts of it), a wide flight of steps down to the Thames ran horizontally to the river. Around 1860 these made way for an embankment wall, giving more space for Black Rod's garden and necessitating this new flight of steps, not with a sentry box at the top as one might suppose but merely a porch. Restored in 1998, it is matched by a similar flight at the Speaker's Green end of the Palace.

Black Rod, the chief executive of the House of Lords, makes little use of his steps; they are so named simply because they lead from the river jetty to his garden. The steps do see occasional use. If a peer is married in the Palace, the couple frequently choose to escape the reception in a launch from the foot of the steps, while every June the pupils of Westminster School row up to the steps, moor and climb up to a cream tea provided for them on the terrace of the House of Lords.

Chelsea Houseboats, Cheyne Walk, Chelsea

The Chelsea Yacht & Boat Co. was founded in 1935 as a boatyard in Battersea Reach, off Cheyne Walk. Very much a working yard, it spent the war years converting craft for military uses, particularly landing craft for D-Day. Many of them were brought back here for repair, and by 1946 one or two people were finding it convenient to stay overnight on the boats. Pretty soon they were being decked out in raffish colours, potted plants were making an appearance and the CY&B Co. found themselves playing the role of waterlords. There is now a powerful sense of community on the houseboats moored here; they even have their own postcode. The only way into this water-world society is to wait for a boat to come on the market; there are mooring permits for a maximum of 58.

College Barge, Cheyne Walk, Chelsea

One of Chelsea's grander houseboats, this started life as a college barge at Cambridge. Rowers who competed against the other university were awarded colours: light blue for Cambridge, dark blue for Oxford, hence a Cambridge (or Oxford) Blue was a hero of some magnitude. Such was the importance of the sport to the two great universities that colleges built their own floating club houses, where crews could change below and watch the races from ther balustraded deck. Somehow this one, formerly the property of New College, Cambridge, quietly slipped its moorings on the Cam and wound up on the Thames as a private house.

Yogurt, **Nine Elms Marina**

The Nine Elms Marina is a high falutin' name for an assembly of houseboats, several of which have seen better days, moored just downstream from the derelict Battersea Power Station. The oddest is Yogurt, a four-masted catamaran designed in the 1960s as an experimental sailing ship. She seemed to want to capsize a lot, so her owner figured she would be happier living out her life as a houseboat. The twin curved pontoons are reminiscent of bananas, and indeed the other boat owners in the marina call her 'The Banana Boat', ignoring her dignified proper name of *Yogurt*.

Serpentine Lodge, Hyde Park

During George IV's brief reign there were many alterations and improvements to Hyde Park. The Serpentine Bridge was built and all the roads and drives were improved. New lodges were built at the Cumberland, Grosvenor, Stanhope and Hyde Park Corner gates. Serpentine Lodge was built in 1829. In the nineteenth century Hyde Park was the fashionable place for Londoners to promenade.

The Ranger of the Royal Parks is an office which was not always the prime ambition of its holder. Rangers have included the Duke of Cambridge, Sir Robert Walpole and Lord Euston. Executive control of the parks later passed to the Commissioners of Woods and Forests, and then to the Commissioner of Works – in the 1930s Lord Lansbury was notably energetic in this role. The Royal Parks Agency now has a Chief Executive, and the agency is based in the Old Police House in the centre of the park. The RPA likes to keep its buildings used and loved, and Serpentine Lodge is now lived in by the Outer Parks manager.

New Lodge, Hyde Park

This is the only standing souvenir of Grant's Folly, or Kensington House, a mansion of prodigious size built between 1872 and 1881 in Prince of Wales Terrace for Albert Grant, company promoter and MP for Kidderminster. So rich and influential was Mr Grant that he had the head gardener's lodge in Kensington Gardens demolished because it interfered with the view of the gardens from his new house; to replace the lodge he built this three-storeyed villa containing some 13 rooms in 1877. It is now enjoyed by the estate manager for the Royal Parks.

The lodge was partly destroyed by a German bomb in 1940, and damaged again in the Great Gale of 1987. Nevertheless it has proved more durable than Grant's Folly. That cost a staggering £300,000 to build, and in the process Grant evicted 1,200 tenants of a tenement called Jennings Rents in order to build himself a seven-acre garden. On completion Grant threw a lavish party, decided not to move in and the house was torn down the following year, in 1882.

Orleans House Octagon, Twickenham

Orleans House acquired its name in 1800 when the exiled Duc d'Orléans came to live here. However, the real creator of the now vanished house and gardens and this sophisticated octagon was James Johnston, Secretary of State for Scotland from 1692 until 1696, when he was dismissed by William III because 'the freedom of his manners was rather disgusting'. Although he returned to office under Queen Anne as the first Secretary of State after Scotland was united with England and Wales in the 1707 Act of Union, Johnston became increasingly preoccupied with his Twickenham house and garden. He was a passionate gardener; as his neighbour Lady Isabella Wentworth commented in her individual style: 'Sure he must have a vast estate to entertain soe many and he has an aboandenc of men at work in the grownd before his hous, I see six or seven diggin; it will be a sweet place when he has don, for I thought it very fyne before.'

The Octagon is all that remains of Johnston's original palace, which had been built by John James in 1710. The Octagon was completed by the architect James Gibbs in 1721, and in August 1729 Johnston entertained Queen Caroline to dinner in it. The house was pulled down in 1927. Nellie Ionides, the daughter of Lord Bearsted, stepped in and saved the Octagon for £250, willing it to the local council 'to be preserved as a place of national interest' and as an art gallery.

Bayer's Folly,
Liphook Crescent, Sydenham

'Sydenham has no history,' wrote
James Thorne disparagingly in
1876, and no doubt this inspired
Charles Bayer, a German
corsetière, to create a little piece
of his own. He came to London
from Nassau, Germany as a
teenager, and started a corset and
stay manufactory which made his
fortune. His son Horace was
knighted, a street in the City was
named Bayer Street (built over
after the Second World War) and
he became the model of the
successful immigrant. To crown
his achievements, he built this
very late folly tower in about 1890
at the top of his garden at
Tewkesbury Lodge, which stood in
Honor Oak Road. The tower is built
of a lovely ochre ironstone rubble,
highlighted with grey stone quoins.
It is 340 feet above the level of
the Thames and offers exceptional
views of London for its private
owner. Tewkesbury Lodge was
demolished in 1930 when Liphook
Crescent was laid out.

Grotto Cottage, Stamford Brook Road, Hammersmith

Bordering the high Victorian enclave of Bedford Park, the little area of Stamford Brook and Starch Green straddles the Chiswick/ Hammersmith borders. The flat open land above the river was well suited to brickfields to feed London's voracious demand. When bricks are heated too long or too high they blacken, burn and twist, and are unsaleable except to those of a creative mind who can see possibilities the ordinary man cannot. The builders of Belgravia, using clean London stock (then covering them with stucco), would have thrown them out without a second thought, but stockbroker James Cubitt used the burnt bricks to great effect in building in 1838 this tiny north-facing cottage. The architect Judith Bottomley restored it in the 1970s. There never was a grotto; the burnt brick and clinker just give the effect of a grotto entrance.

The Stables, Rylett Road, Hammersmith

A street away from Grotto Cottage is a bizarre building known as The Stables, all castellations and wild fenestration, a niche with a statue (this part of London was strongly Roman since the foundation of a Catholic school here in the late seventeenth century) and poky little towers. It was converted into a house by the architect Peter Faggetter in the 1990s, and the owners have now blighted the façade with visually obtrusive security grilles behind all the windows. The Stables would seem to have been built c.1878 by the Jonadab Hanks, who lived here at the time.

Royal Naval College Gates, Greenwich

The Royal Naval Hospital complex at Greenwich
is the most majestic group of buildings in
London, grander than any palace, containing
buildings by Inigo Jones, John Webb,
Christopher Wren, Nicholas Hawksmoor and
James Stuart. Unlike its inspiration, the Army's
Royal Hospital Chelsea, it has not housed
service pensioners since 1869, becoming in
1873 the home of the Royal Naval College.
These remarkable gates were built in 1834 to
commemorate Admiral Anson's three-year,
nine-month foray round the globe in 1740–4,
during which he captured the Spanish galleon
Acapulco and came away with £500,000, at a
time when £500 would have built a most
luxurious mansion. Anson managed to keep
most of it, as a visit to his brother's house
at Shugborough in Staffordshire will show.
The great 6-foot diameter globes on top of the
gates represent the terrestrial and celestial
spheres, but the iron bands have rusted and
it is now impossible to decipher them. They
cost the prodigious sum of 40 guineas each.

Old Royal Observatory, Greenwich

On the spot where time begins is this high-windowed, north-facing octagonal room; this is Flamsteed House, the original Greenwich Observatory building. It consists of a small dwelling on the ground floor with a fine octagonal room above, built by Sir Christopher Wren in brick and wood dressed to look like stone for John Flamsteed, the Derbyshire-born first Astronomer Royal. The Government gave him a home and an observatory but no instrument to observe with, so after eight unobservant years he finally built his own telescope in 1683.

The foundation stone was laid on 10 August 1675, and as this was effectively the birth of the building Flamsteed amused himself by drawing up its horoscope. Astrologists argue this shows that the great astronomer was secretly an astrologist, conveniently ignoring his inscription on the chart *Risum teneatis amici*? (Can you keep from laughing, my friends?).

The strange pole and ball on the left is the red time-ball, dropped daily at 1pm so sailors in the Thames could set their chronometers by sight – the sound of a cannon would travel too slowly for accuracy.

**Steel half-timbered house,
Banstock Road, Burnt Oak**

Half timbering (more correctly timber framing) has been the ultimate aspiration of a certain segment of the English middle class. If the genuine article is not available, they will simply pretend. This half-timbered beauty on the Watling Estate is built of metal; surplus production facilities at the end of the First World War meant that the aircraft factories' production lines were rejigged to turn out metal walls – swords into ploughshares. Living in a metal house has its problems – broiling in summer, rust instead of rising damp, frozen in winter, and how does one hang a picture? But these have been standing for over seventy years, and many of the former council tenants have bought their houses, and, in this case, stuck-on half-timbering and 'tree'.

The Watling Estate was known to the existing inhabitants of Hendon and Burnt Oak as 'Little Moscow', because of the anticipated political affiliations of the incomers from London's East End, who were being rehoused here from their slum tenements in 'homes fit for heroes' by the London County Council in the 1920s.

Rustic Toolshed, Soho Square

In February 1886 the inhabitants of Soho Square had just spent £200 on improvements and refused to open it to the public; gone was the statue which stood in the middle of the square, either Charles II or the Duke of Monmouth – no one was quite sure which – removed by Frederick Goodall RA to adorn his garden in Harrow Weald. (The statue, corroded by the London air, has now been returned.) Before that there had been a fountain with four jets, representing the Thames, the Severn, the Tyne and the Humber, which was filled in and became a flower-bed, the fate of many fountains. It was replaced by an octagonal building to form a tool-house and summer-house, and over a hundred years later the architect S. J. Thacker's rural curio still survives to fulfil the first function.

Crooms Hill Gazebo, Greenwich

The Welsh word Cromlech means 'crooked stone'. The root 'crom' has been used here since time immemorial: Crooms Hill, or crooked hill, was mentioned by name in 918 when the land was granted to the abbey of Ghent – the road has always had the same name, which probably makes it the oldest named road in the London area. This gazebo on the wall of The Grange was designed by Robert Hooke in 1672 for Sir William Hooker, who was Lord Mayor of London in 1673–4, and memorably dismised by Pepys as 'a plain ordinary silly man, but rich'. Inside, the domed ceiling has fine plasterwork of leaves and berries.

Queen Anne's Alcove, Hyde Park

This grandly splendid Corinthian portico, a rare garden building from Wren, was built in 1705 to replace a summer-house by his rival William Talman and to answer the vista down Dial Walk in the Queen's Garden at Kensington Palace but after a while it became infested with 'undesirable personages' who decided it was a fine place in which to sleep. By the mid-nineteenth century the situation had become intolerable to the Commissioner of Works, in whose charge the security of the Royal Parks was vested. In 1867 a builder named Cowley magnanimously offered to move it at his own expense, so it was transferred to its present position by Lancaster Gate.

Princess Amelia's Temple, Gunnersbury Park, Brentford

In the mid-eighteenth century scores of brick temples with wooden porticos were thrown up on every gentleman's estate. Standing by the round pond in Gunnersbury Park is this rare London survival, with three classical reliefs inside. The now rather municipal park had a distinguished pedigree: it was created by Princess Amelia, the second daughter of George II, to rival Kew, yet she ignored the Chinese and Moorish architectural fashions over the river. Amelia's follies were classical and Gothick. Most have disappeared, leaving just this Doric Temple or Dairy. It is thought to have been built by Sir William Chambers, who also built the Pagoda at Kew.

Temple of Bellona, Kew Gardens

In 1760 Amelia's sister-in-law Princess Augusta commissioned Sir William Chambers to build temples for her across the river in the gardens at Kew Palace. Chambers responded with a temple to Aeolus, the god of the winds, another to Arethusa, a nymph of Diana who was transformed into a fountain, and this grander Temple of Bellona, the Roman goddess of war, sister and wife of Mars. The interior has an oval domed room with names and numbers of British and Hanoverian regiments which fought in the Seven Years War.

Queen Charlotte's Cottage, Kew Gardens

Between bearing fifteen children by George III, Queen Charlotte designed this simple and satisfactory thatched brick cottage in 1772. It was built in the grounds of Ormonde Lodge, which had been laid out by William Bridgman with follies and garden buildings by William Kent, including the now legendary Merlin's Cave, one of the earliest Gothick follies. All these were destroyed in 1765 when the gardens were relandscaped by Lancelot 'Capability' Brown, and they are now incorporated into Kew Gardens. Inside the cottage is a room covered with Hogarth prints, and a room upstairs has flowery murals, said to be by Princess Elizabeth.

Oak Cottage, Chiswick Mall
This 1810 cottage on the riverside was built on a foundation of oyster shells, and the high garden wall and watertight glass screen above are strictly utilitarian. The present owners have seen people swimming past the front door during higher tides.

Cottages, Addison Place, Kensington
Thirty years after these cottages were built, they were humble dwellings, but a century and a half later, due purely to their location in one of London's more fashionable districts, they have assumed an elegance which their understated architecture allows. Maps of the 40-acre Norland Estate on which they stand show this little Regency-style row was built after 1822 and before 1848, almost certainly by the developer Charles Richardson as servants' quarters for his grand houses in Addison Avenue. Richardson bought the estate in 1839, went bankrupt in 1855 and was next heard of in Glasgow as a dealer in patent medicines. They stand in a half-moon mews behind Royal Crescent, facing a terrace of 1960s white-painted houses, which compare unfavourably with this enchanting composition opposite, showing how it should be done.

Cottage, Clareville Grove, South Kensington
This quaint wistaria-covered house, sheltered
by a fig-tree, is the kind of survivor that
enhances London, despite some eyesores in the
street such as the petrol station opposite. This
was the first house in the street, which was
originally built as Gloucester Grove West by
developer William Blake. He leased the cottage
to John Sparham, a carpenter, in 1826.
Blake's development of irregular, small houses
gives these streets a pleasantly organic,
villagey atmosphere. The road was renamed
after the nearby Clareville Cottage, the
home of the 1840s singer Jenny Lind, 'the
Swedish Nightingale'.

Elystan Place, Chelsea

The resident baroness stoutly defends her jungly façade against charges of eccentricity. She inherited a collection of exotic birds and was forced to find a rapid solution to their housing problem. This apparent tropical rainforest actually consists of a Himalayan cherry tree, an aspen, a May tree, apple trees, and a pink chestnut artfully woven with silk mimosas to train the birds in 'homing'.

Gordon Place, Kensington

Formerly known as Orchard Street, Gordon Place was given these facing terraces of three-storey houses in 1846 by Charles and Frederick Sewell of Paddington for artisans. By the time of the 1851 census several instances of multiple occupancy were recorded. Coachmen and grooms from Kensington Palace were put up here, in what was very much a working-class environment. Instead of extending the road to the end of the cul-de-sac, the space has been filled up with front gardens with a narrow pathway running down the middle. This provides its residents with an elegant and secluded retreat.

Hawksmoor Conduit, Greenwich Park

Underneath Greenwich Park is a warren of tunnels, criss-crossing each other. These are said to be conduits, and indeed as far back as 1268 there are accounts for repairs to the conduits supplying the buildings in Greenwich with water. Christopher Wren was recorded as having repaired 'the underground passages, or conduits' in 1700. Several of the conduits were abandoned in 1732. And yet these conduits are remarkably well built for the simple service of water supply to a few wealthy households. In the nineteenth century a park-keeper wrote 'That many of the passages in the Park were for the conveying of water we will not dispute, but it is difficult to imagine why so elaborate a construction ... where two persons can walk side by side without stooping, should have been formed for such a purpose.' We can only speculate.

It is not certain that Nicholas Hawksmoor designed this stately, solitary building in the Park, but as Clerk of Works to Greenwich Hospital from 1698 to 1735, assisting first Wren during the repair of the tunnels, then Vanbrugh, and having particular responsibility for the conduits, it seems likely.

St Botolph's Church Hall, Bishopsgate Churchyard, City of London

Hidden away behind Liverpool Street station is a parish hall. It was built in 1861, and the two painted figures of charity children in the niches either side of the door stand on plinths clearly labelled 'Coade Sealey 1821'. These are not their names, but the brand name of a remarkable, artificial stone with excellent weathering properties created by a Mrs Coade. They were brought here from the earlier parish hall in Peter Street.

Spencer Water Tower, Arthur Road, Wimbledon

'Earl Spencer, for the preservation of his noble manor-house at Wimbledon against fire, and to be well supplied with water, ordered a well to be dug at some distance from the house, to the amazing depth of near 600 feet: it was begun the 31st of May last year [1796], and on Saturday, the man who was first employed upon the undertaking, gave the signal to the person above to draw him up, as he had found the spring, and was immersed in water so deep that his life became endangered. This was at eleven o'clock in the morning, and at three in the afternoon the fluid rose to 350 feet: and during Sunday and yesterday, its increase was more than a foot an hour; the water, proceeding from a rock, is remarkably sweet; and from the strata it passes through, is strongly impregnated with mineralic qualities. This valuable concern has already cost his Lordship two thousand pounds, but will fully recompense him by its utility; as, before this well was finished, the only supplies for the family were either rain falling during the wet weather, or water which the servants procured from the adjoining fish-ponds.'

A year later, in 1798, Spencer built this mighty octagonal domed well-house above the spring which has outlasted his Henry Holland-designed home. It was converted into a house in 1975, 26 years after the mansion it served was demolished.

Shakespeare Temple, Hampton Court Road, Hampton

The great eighteenth-century actor David Garrick was a passionate advocate of the genius of William Shakespeare, who was then not as widely appreciated as now. He commissioned Roubiliac to sculpt a statue of the Bard and had this elegant octagonal Ionic temple on the riverside built to hold it. It would appear that Roubiliac himself designed the frame for his jewel. The statue is now in the British Museum, but the little temple has not been forgotten – in 1998 the Temple Trust restored the building, commissioned a £60,000 replica of the statue and reinstated the Swan of Avon inside on a scagliola plinth.

Avenue House Dovecote, Finchley

'Inky' Stephens never minded his nickname; Stephen's Ink provided him with a substantial fortune which he spent on improving his north London estate. He commissioned an Italian architect to extend and beautify his house in Finchley, and in the picturesquely landscaped grounds he assembled an impressive arboretum. At the eastern end of the grounds he built in the 1870s a bizarre concrete structure known as The Bothy, possibly the first concrete building in Britain since the Roman White Tower at Dover Castle, but now languishing forgotten and overgrown. In a more lighthearted mood came this elegant dovecote by the stable block, a turreted touch of the Loire Valley in Finchley. Stephens's Italianate villa, surprisingly not listed by English Heritage, is now owned by the local council and the park is open to the public.

New River Walk Bothy, Canonbury

The New River was the creation of one man, Sir Hugh Myddelton, who in 1609 embarked on his grandiose plan to bring fresh drinking water to London by siphoning off one of the tributaries of the River Lea before it became too polluted on its way to the Thames. Astonishingly he succeeded, and the New River Company flourished until the twentieth century when it was incorporated into the Thames Water Company. In addition to benefiting hundreds of thousands of Londoners, he created a visual amenity which his successors have beautified through the centuries – the most sublime corner of Hertfordshire is at Great Amwell, the source of the New River, with tiny islets on a shady pool with urns, monuments and inscriptions praising the work of Sir Hugh.

In Islington a stretch of the New River has been revitalised with lottery money so that it now meanders through a small park. Also refurbished is this tiny round conical-roofed hut, now a gardener's shed.

Gauging Locks, Brentford

'Squalid and uninviting as is Brentford, it is redeemed by the vicinity of the little stream from which it takes its name, the Brent.' This comment in an 1893 guide to London was obviously written before the stream was turned into a canal. Clearly seen from Brentford Bridge, here is an important manned pair of locks on London's canals, where boats can enter the Grand Union system from the Thames. Nearby is a large bonded warehouse where cargoes could be weighed. A gauging lock is where this can be done by fastening a float within a tube which shows the amount of freeboard between the gunwhales and water level.

Half Tide Lock and Weir, Richmond

When the new London Bridge was built in 1832 (the one that now graces Lake Havasu, near Las Vegas), the size of its piers had a disastrous effect upstream, reducing the river between Teddington and Richmond to a tidal creek – on several summers the mighty Thames was no more than 18 inches deep at low tide. It was clear that something had to be done to make the river above Richmond non-tidal. After heroic campaigning, led by J. B. Hilditch of Asgill House in Richmond, the Richmond Sluice, Lock and Slipway Act 1890 was passed. The Thames Conservancy then performed an astonishing volte-face; they conceded defeat, spent the then huge sum of £20,000 on the two lock cottages and the superb Victorian ornamental ironwork we see today, and offered to operate the works. Thanks to Mr Hilditch and Mr Stoney, the Irish inventor of the system, a precursor of the Thames Barrier, we still have a river above Richmond.

Windmill, Windmill Road, Wimbledon

Windmills are not as uncommon in the London area as one might expect, although even a hundred years ago their function was tending more to the decorative than the practical. The Wimbledon Windmill was built by Charles March in 1817, but within 80 years it had been made into an eye-catcher. Lord Spencer bought it from the March family in 1864 in an attempt to buy up all the properties on the Common so he could sell it off for building, but local opposition was too strong. Spencer managed to convert the octagonal base of the mill into six tiny cottages. The size of the base nearly dwarfs the windmill above, which was further diminished in size in 1893 when the millpost was removed and it became a *point de vue*. According to the mill's biographer Norman Plastow, it is the only hollow-post flour mill in Britain. The last occupants of the cottages moved out in 1974, leaving a surveyor's delight of dry rot, death watch beetle, longhorn beetle and furniture beetle. The first floor has been converted into the Windmill Museum.

Tile Kiln,
Walmer Road, Notting Hill

It may not look like a house, and it wasn't built as one, but it is now. In the mid-nineteenth century this area was known as the Potteries, and the Survey of London commented that 'the conditions of filth, disease and insanitation in which its inhabitants were found to be living and dying gave the area a notoriety perhaps unsurpassed by any other district in London.' The population density was 130 to the acre; there was no sewerage, simply open cesspits, and over 3,000 pigs roamed free. In 1849 21 inhabitants died of cholera.

The potteries here were started by Ralph Adams in 1827 when there was no other trade in the neighbourhood. This tile kiln was marked on Ordnance Survey maps by 1863, rebuilt in 1879 by Charles Adams and converted into a house by Michael Brown in the 1970s, during the redevelopment of Hippodrome Mews, the only memento of the old Hippodrome Racecourse on the Ladbroke Estate which opened in a welter of publicity in 1837 and quietly closed four years later. Walmer Road was built in 1852 when the area was being sanitised, the year the Duke of Wellington died at Walmer Castle.

**Potomac Tower,
Gunnersbury Park, Brentford**
After Princess Amelia died,
Gunnersbury Park was divided
into three lots. Nathan Meyer
Rothschild bought the largest
section in 1835. In 1861 Lionel
Rothschild bought the southern
part of the park, and transformed
an old claypit into the Potomac
Pond, with matching rockery and
boathouse. The house on the
previous page still looks like
a kiln; it is hard to believe that
the Potomac Tower may have
started life as one. A boarded-up
and castellated octagonal tower
rises with all the required details
(brackets in the form of heads of
medieval kings) in the requisite
places, so the whole effect is
convincingly old. It was built by an
unknown architect as a rather
sumptuous boathouse, and
today it is struggling for survival,
hunched up against the pool,
neglected and vandalized, ignored
and unloved by its owners.

Severndroog Castle,
Castlewood Park, Shooter's Hill

This Building was Erected MDCCLXXXIV by the
Representative of the late S[r.] William James
Bart. To commemorate that Gallant Officer's
Atchievements in the East Indies during his
command of the Company's Marine Forces in
those Seas And in a particular manner to Record
the Conquest of The Castle of Severndroog
off the Coast of Malabar which fell to his superior
Valour and able Conducton the 2nd Day of
April MDCCLV

The 'Representative' was in fact Sir James's widow,
and as befitted a good Company man, the tower was
designed by the East India Company's Surveyor,
Richard Jupp. Sir William's great achievement was
ridding the Goan coast of the notorious pirate
Conojee Angria, who was ensconced in the fortress
of Severndroog on a small, rocky well-fortified island
about a mile in circumference and 'within musket
shot of the mainland'. Despite walls 50 feet high and
18 feet thick, the fort was attacked, burnt and taken
by Commodore James: Angria's navy had had to
land as they were prohibited by their religion from
eating on board.

Summer-house and seat, Radnor Gardens, Twickenham

Radnor House was bombed out in the Second World War, and these two orphaned garden buildings no more than 30 feet apart in a little park between Cross Deep and the Thames are the only relics of the 4th Earl of Radnor's famous mansion. The 1750 summer-house with its elegant ogee arcade was recently restored by the Radnor Gardens Trust, which managed to get the summer-house listed Grade II in 1983, when it was overgrown and vandalized.

Sri India Restaurant, Bishopsgate Churchyard

If ever a building proclaimed its function, this is it: an Ottoman hamam in the heart of the City of Mammon. The fashion for Turkish baths was petering out by the First World War, but somehow this little curiosity, built in 1894–5 by Harold Elphick for James Forder Nevill, survived Hitler's bombs and every other redevelopment scheme and continued as baths until the 1950s. It was triumphantly converted into the Gallipoli Restaurant in the 1980s by, suitably, a Turkish gentleman named Mr Mourat. His lone battle against the pressures of the surrounding developers and encircling demolition work was to be applauded. Now housing an Indian restaurant, this City caravanserai is said to have been based on the nineteenth-century shrine at Jerusalem's Church of the Holy Sepulchre.

Slate House, Blackheath Park

The Georgian redoubt of Blackheath Park is a model for speculative builders. Once the grounds of Wricklemarsh Manor, it was bought in 1783 by John Cator, who came up with the idea of agreeable housing in a parkland setting, a concept developers have been striving to emulate ever since. It is now heresy to criticise Georgian architecture and fashionable to call for the demolition of most thirty-year-old buildings, which makes Patrick Gwynne's 1968 house extremely vulnerable. Among the fine-mortared uniformity of its Georgian surroundings, this slate grey snail of a house, a refugee from the campus of some mid-western university, provides a cool contrast of alternative elegance.

Miramonte Lodge, New Malden

'A Hollywood House in Surrey' enthused the sale particulars when Miramonte in New Malden was put on the market in 1945. It had been built in 1936 by E. Maxwell Fry, and hailed by the *Buildings of England* as the 'English International Modern style at its most flamboyant and inventive'. For all its modernity, this is effectively the Coach House, a three-car garage with 'The Chauffeur's Flat' above, with living-room, two bedrooms, kitchen, bathroom and balcony.

The English appreciate new houses and love old houses, but have little time for second-hand houses. In 1946 Miramonte was crudely divided into four flats, and not reunited as one house for ten years. Since the late 1950s it has been owned by one family, the Barkis, and now clearly carries the weight of its sixty-odd years.

Danson Road, Bexley

In the 1930s Mr D. C. Wadhwa from Multan in India (now in Pakistan) was practising as an architect with an office in Imperial House, Regent Street. He secured a commission from the builders Martin & Co of Sidcup to design ten villas and he rose magnificently to the challenge, producing a row of astonishingly modern houses along the road facing Danson Park. Derivative they may have been, but they were in the vanguard of architectural thought for the time, and the first brave purchasers had bought the last word in modernity. Unfortunately for Mr Wadhwa there were not enough brave purchasers. The burghers of Bexley wanted Tudorbethan like the rest of suburban England. 'If there are any contravenes to the by-laws I shall be very pleased to amend these plans accordingly,' wrote Mr. Wadhwa despairingly, uncomprehendingly, in 1935 but to no avail; Martins were turning to Frederick Jones, a more conventional designer, to complete the commission. The pioneer treads a lonely road.

One or two of the present occupants are aware of the brilliance of their homes; none knew they were designed by an Indian architect; most are trying to install plastic windows before somebody comes along and lists them.

Gazebo, Kensington

Gazebos are not common in London, but surely the Victorian architect Joel Bray slipped up when he omitted to place this elegant little Gothicism as a finial to developer John Inderwick's black and white stuccoed terraces. John Inderwick was a snuff box importer, an unlikely trade in which to make a fortune, but he left £100,000 and his firm was still operating as a tobacconists over a hundred years later. This tiny copper-roofed summer-house was built to complete one of his terraces, echoing the main house's stair turret dome built by a Corfiot astronomer and painter, Spiridone Gambardella, when he lived here in the 1850s.

Oddly enough the first recorded mention of the word 'gazebo' appeared in 1750, in W. & J. Halfpenny's pattern book *New Designs for Chinese Temples, etc.*; oddly, because the great time for gazebo building was in the previous century, when they were simply known as pavilions or summer-houses. Nobody really knows the origin of the word; some believe it to be a corruption of a forgotten Chinese term; others speculate on a literary joke, taking the word 'gaze' and adding a cod Latin suffix to make a sham verb: 'I gaze about.'

Gazebo, Richmond
Marked on early estate maps as a 'Bathing House', this mid-eighteenth-century castellated white stucco summer-house stands away from the river in the grounds of Trumpeter's House. The Thames was formerly much wider than it is today. The great bulk of Richmond Palace was torn down during the Commonwealth, and Trumpeter's House was built on part of the site for the diplomat Richard Hill in 1702, named after two medieval figures of trumpeters on the ancient Middle Gate of the palace.

Air Vent, King Edward's Memorial Park, Wapping

This elegant rotunda set in a quiet park on the north bank of the river is purely functional, unlike most rotundas in parks. It was constructed in 1905 as an air vent for Rotherhithe Tunnel. After studying the swirling abstract Art Nouveau ironwork on the grilles of the rotunda for a while, the initials LCC – for the old London County Council – gradually come into focus. Although cars were an increasingly common sight on London's roads by this time, the huge bulk of the city's traffic was still horse-drawn, and these vents were necessary to allow the air in the tunnel to remain breathable – not because of noxious exhaust fumes from horseless carriages, but from the sheer volume of horse manure. The pavements either side of the carriageway were not for pedestrians, but for men with spades collecting the dung.

Warehouse, Alexandra Bridge, Clink Street SE1

Alexandra Bridge is guaranteed to baffle any London cabbie, because it is far better known as the Cannon Street railway bridge. These grandly sinister Diocletian windows speak of mysterious doings, and when the Thames tour boats point to the Clink Prison, a shiver of ancient terror runs down the most blasé tourist's spine. Unfortunately Clink Prison, the debtors' prison which for centuries defined gaol, was burnt down in the Gordon Riots in 1780. It stood on a site a little further back from the riverside, now occupied by a tourist museum, while the warehouse under the railway bridge was designed and built by Sir John Hawkshaw, the consulting engineer to the South Eastern Railway. Work started in 1863 and it was completed by 1866. It now houses building materials for a local contractor.

The Mayflower, Rotherhithe Street, Rotherhithe

There is a wonderful view of Tower Bridge from the riverside balcony of this apparently ancient pub. There is said to have been an inn here since the sixteenth century, originally called The Shippe, then the Spreadeagle & Crown, until the influx of American visitors prompted an adroit change of name to The Mayflower. The Pilgrim Fathers started from hereabouts (before stopping off at Plymouth) in 1611. As the last stop on the river before reaching the estuary, the pub sells stamps as well as beer, through custom rather than right. It was bombed in 1940 and rebuilt in the style of a seventeenth-century Thames-side inn, 'a picturesque pastiche,' commented Pevsner.

Tyburn Cottage, Grosvenor Road, Pimlico

Looking like a slice from some vast square post-modern wedding cake, Tyburn Cottage perches on the vestigial edge of Pimlico before it falls into the Thames. Pimlico's curious name is allegedly derived from a landlord called Ben Pimlico from Hoxton, on the northern border of the City, whose beer was so good that rival establishments sprang up on London's periphery using his name. Underneath the cottage is a huge arched entrance, visible only at low tide, which explains the name of the cottage – this is the outlet of the River Tyburn.

Leaning Tower, Rotherhithe

A hithe in Old English was a landing-place on a river, while Rother was the old term for oxen. So this was the river port for landing cattle. A little further upstream was the landing place for sheep, Lamb Hithe, now mutated to Lambeth. For many years the Leaning Tower of Rotherhithe was the premises of Braithwaite & Dean, a barge company. They had a large sign on the waterfront, and lightermen used to pull up here to collect their wages. Undistinguished architecturally, it stood out as the tallest building in a once absurdly picturesque row of largely wooden tenements fronting the Thames, seedy in the extreme but vibrantly populated in the 1950s by a bohemian set of artists and writers. The row was pulled down in the 1960s by the council as a health hazard. No one can remember why this building, out of all the rest, was reprieved. This is now one of the most solitary private houses in London, and certainly the only place where one can play the trumpet at 2am without fear of disturbing the neighbours.

Gothick Lodge, Phipps Bridge Road, Morden

Why is Gothick sometimes spelt with a 'K'?
It refers to the highly decorative secular Gothic
revived in the early eighteenth century and
championed by Horace Walpole and his
Committee of Taste. As Walpole was one of
society's leading commentators, his word had
more effect than today's planning officers;
one acerbic word was enough to destroy any
budding reputation. The surprise is that for
such an idiosyncratic and easily dated style,
two out of the three buildings pictured here
date from the late twentieth century.

Number 98a is a tiny mustard-coloured
Gothick castle with an octagonal turret at the
rear towering up to 20 feet high. For years
it was a romantic ivy-covered ruin, until
it was restored in the 1980s by the National
Trust in an unusually light-hearted and
frivolous mood, even to the extent of adding
the tiny prospect tower at the back.

Gothick House, Kew Foot Road, Richmond

It's hard to disguise the location of this little Gothick bauble, but serious
overplanting has obscured its original eye-catcher intent. This was a house to
be seen – the towering pinnacles, the decorative battlements, the boldly
incised windows – but now net-curtained modesty requires a planted screen.

Gypsy Tower, Gypsy Hill
Christ Church Gypsy Hill
as built by John Giles
in 1862 was burnt down in
1982, but its mighty tower
remains and where the
nave once stood are now
two smaller modern
towers thrusting up
against the revived
Perpendicular of their old
redundant parent. The
views across London from
the top of the tower high
on the hill are immense,
which prompted a
developer to snuggle the
two new towers together
with the old one to create
an ideal home. Inside
there is marble and a lift.

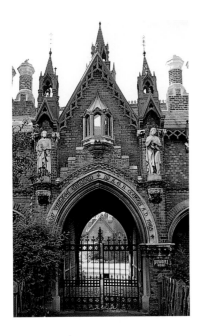

Highgate Cemetery Lodge, Highgate Cemetery
London's finest, most romantic, eeriest, burial ground was created in 1838 by the London Cemetery Company, laid out in 17 acres on the side of Highgate Hill, one of the best locations in the city, by Stephen Geary, the architect J. B. Bunning and the landscape architect David Ramsey. The chapel lodge at the entrance, probably by Bunning, was accurately described by a Victorian writer as 'Undertaker's Gothic'. When it was first built it had a tall two-storeyed bell-tower cupola on its roof. The tombs, crypts, mausolea and funerary avenues of Highgate Cemetery have been preserved from the hand of the developer by the Friends of Highgate Cemetery, one of the most pro-active conservation groups in the country. Some of the designs for death are breathtaking: see the Egyptian Avenue, and at a cost of £5,000 the mausoleum of Julius Beer (1836–80), which copied the the tomb of King Mausolus at ancient Halicarnassus, now the resort of Bodrum.

Holly Village, Highgate, *left* and *above*
Situated next to Highgate Cemetery – innocently reinforcing the association of the Gothic style of architecture with Horror – this little enclave of some sixteen houses, jealously guarded by its inhabitants, was designed by H. A. Darbishire for Angela Burdett-Coutts, a fantastically rich Victorian lady with a well-developed social conscience. This was the cutting edge of 1855 architecture, breathtakingly modern for its day, cleverly designed and ingeniously thought out.

Aldridge Lodge, Aldridge Road Villas, North Kensington

Here is an example to show that contemporary private housing doesn't have to be expensive or outrageous or a pastiche of earlier styles; this little house, never built as a lodge, takes small elements of modern architecture and assembles them unselfconsciously and effectively to provide a clean and sympathetic addition to the Victorian street. The pronounced gable is the only concession to retro taste, and because one enters in at the first floor, with the main bulk of the house below pavement level, it is much roomier than it at first appears.

Britten Street, Chelsea

This tiny worker's cottage could not have been expected to last for much longer when the construction of James Savage's lusty new parish church of St Luke's took place across the road in 1824. It shyly kept its place when the Duke of Wellington's brother was installed as the first rector; it was overlooked when Charles Dickens was married there, but through world wars and centuries this dear little house has tenaciously survived to become a much dearer little house, thanks to its location at the heart of Chelsea.

The Temple, Edwardes Square, Kensington

In 1811 William Edwardes, 2nd Lord Kensington did a deal with Louis Léon Changeur to develop 11 acres of his land south of Kensington High Street. Changeur was a mysterious character who came to London in 1804, spent a little time in jail for being French, and by 1810 was practising as an architect in Great Russell Street. Edwardes Square was odd from the start. Changeur was over generous with open space, allowing 3 acres for the gardens, which meant the quarters round the square were unusually small. This may have been the reason that the houses in the square did not sell as quickly as expected. As a result in 1813 Changeur was declared bankrupt, and fled back to France.

The square was laid out in 1814–20 'in groups and winding walks, in a manner different from most other squares' by Agostino Alio, who lived at No. 15. In June 1820 George Ledwell Taylor, later to be the architect of the fantastic May's Folly at Hadlow in Kent, wrote 'The Temple is nearly finished and the Accounts passed, which argues he was the designer, although the outline of a similar building appears on Changeur's masterplan of 1812. A plaque on the side of the temple, now a house for the gardener, gives a potted history of the square. Outside is an ancient water pump; the railing uprights round the square are topped with pineapple finials.

Stag Lodge, Wimbledon

Lodges were designed to sing the wealth and influence of the owner of the great house and to act as a guardhouse, perpetually on the lookout for miscreants and undesirables, but when these necessary functions are stripped away the lodge has to struggle to find its role. This tiny stuccoed lodge led to Earl Spencer's Wimbledon Park House, now demolished. The hedge, planted to stop us looking in, now prevents the occupants from looking out. The stag has now disappeared from the roof, temporarily it is to be hoped.

Hanover Gate Lodge, Regent's Park, *left*
Besides John Nash's terraces around Regent's Park
are other, smaller buildings sometimes of greater
architectural merit. At Hanover Gate, this heavily
rusticated small baroque lodge has such chamfered
corners that it is usually taken to be octagonal,
following the roof line. Swaggering volutes, a tall
central chimney and huge projecting porches all
offer far more architecture than necessary for such
a small house; one can sense that Nash had fun
with this building. He would have been appalled
at the way its effect is muted by street furniture.

Regent's Park was a master plan by Nash, who
created the park and its surrounding houses. He
worked on this huge scheme – London's only major
piece of centralized planning – from 1812 to 1827.
The speed with which his proposals were accepted
led to some speculation about the relationship
between his attractive wife Mary Anne and the
Prince Regent.

Asgill House, Richmond
Many of the buildings pictured in this book were immaculately conceived without the aid
of an architect. None demonstrates the spectacular heights of elegance and intelligence
which can be achieved by an architect at the peak of his powers more clearly than Asgill
House in Richmond, built as a summer retreat for Sir Charles Asgill, a Lord Mayor of
London, by Sir Robert Taylor and completed in 1762. In the late nineteenth century, when
it was described as 'a sound and pleasing old structure', it was the residence of
J. B. Hilditch, who fought for the Richmond Half Tide Lock and Weir, and today it remains
a private house, leased by an American from the Crown Estates for the past thirty
years. The house must be as satisfying internally as it is externally; only three families
have lived here in the past 120 years.

Buttress Castle, Phipps Bridge Road, Morden

The National Trust is the owner of this strange piece of south-west London whimsy. A Mr Everett, who lived in nearby Wandle Villa, began building riverside cottages for his workers in the 1820s; when more staff necessitated more housing, he simply added to the terrace. Such haphazard planning had its inevitable consequence – having failed to take the water table into account, the northern end of the terrace began to sink into the sodden flood plain of the Wandle. Urgent action was needed, and Mr. Everett rose magnificently to the occasion. Instead of a dull, conventional buttress to prop up the end of the terrace, he created a final cottage, one up, two down, with a spiral staircase, all neatly clothed in a castellated flint skin and ruinated battlements.

One cottage in the row used to be an ale house, and in the late nineteenth century workers at the nearby William Morris factory were housed in the terrace. Each house had its own bridge over the River Wandle to an island where the privies stood. The cottages were flooded twice a year until the National Trust diverted the course of the river.

Fanlight Cottage, Oakley Road, Bromley
The inspiration behind this front window in a pleasant early Victorian villa is unknown, but it was put it in in the early 1970s.

Langford Place, St John's Wood

John Adams was an eminent Victorian figurative sculptor who, tired of being mistaken for other John Adamses, appropriated the name of his birthplace and reinvented himself as John Adams-Acton. He was befriended by William Gladstone and sculpted many of the wealthy notables of the day, from Disraeli to Dickens, from Pope Leo XIII to Landseer. His chef d'oeuvre was a mighty statue of Sir Titus Salt, erected by the Town Hall in Bradford. Not, one might think, much to the taste of Maurice and Doris Saatchi, who once owned this house. With the lavish commissions he earned he created this extraordinary prickly little cottage for his sister, crouched in its yard, now further hemmed in by high walls and modern blocks of flats peering down at it, twin thin gables screaming its independence. Even the bay window looks armoured, as if some giant alien insect had attempted to construct a human dwelling. Underneath the window is a plaque with an inscription from John xvii, 21:

'That they all may be one as thou, Father, art in me and I in thee, that thay also may be one in us: that the world may believe that Thou hast sent me.'

St Alban's Church Tower, Wood Street, City of London

Living in a vertical pile on the middle of a traffic island outside a police station and overlooked on all sides by office workers may not be everyone's idea of heaven, but if one works in the City and simply needs a place with some character to lay one's head at night, then St Alban's Wood Street could be the answer. Certainly somebody thinks so, because this former church tower has been converted into a miniature fortress, sealed off against the outside world. The medieval church was rebuilt in Gothic style in 1633, burnt down in the Great Fire of London, rebuilt in 1682–5 by Sir CHristopher Wren and finally destroyed by bombing in 1940; after the rubble was cleared away and the ruins finally demolished, the old tower stood there for several years until it was converted into a private house.

Horniman Museum Tower, London Road, Lewisham

Sometimes said to be the only example of Richardsonian Romanesque in Britain, this is in fact a wonderfully inventive and superbly executed piece of pure Arts and Craftsmanship, an English Art Nouveau. The clock-tower of the Horniman Free Museum, one of the most eclectic and enjoyable museums in London, rises up 120 feet, square, solid and beautiful, transforming itself slowly and elegantly into a round tower with four corner turrets. It is the masterpiece of Harrison Townsend, the architect of the Whitechapel Art Gallery, and his enlightened patron, the tea millionaire Frederick Horniman.

Chapel in the Woods, Strawberry Hill, Twickenham

Strawberry Hill 'now has an air of shabby dilapidation; the old Gothic tricks and devices of its brilliant owner are now revealed like old scenery viewed by daylight. It offers a good specimen of that amateur "Gothic" once found in every castle and villa, with its tower, spire, "bays", all in right lath and plaster. Within are all the rooms and corners which were the delight of the rather feminine owner,' wrote Percy Fitzgerald sternly in 1893. The wheel has turned, and so has the function of this sham chapel, built for the 'rather feminine' Horace Walpole by John Chute and Thomas Gayfere in 1772–4. All façade and no substance, the little folly was built to show off Walpole's collection of stained glass and to house a shrine brought from Rome, but when Strawberry Hill was taken over by the Catholic St Mary's College the 'chapel' was consecrated. A rare example of a sham becoming real.

Brompton Cemetery Lodge, Earl's Court
Stephen Geary was a man of many interests: sculptor, inventor, drinker, architect and cemetery designer. Employed by the West of London & Westminster Cemetery Co. in 1836, he was sacked when the company accepted Benjamin Baud's grandiose classical design in 1840.
A triumphal arch, a Bath stone colonnade above catacombs, an octagonal domed chapel: the effects were as impressive as any stage set, but the quality of work was not up to the impossibly high standards of the company, and Baud was sacked and sued in 1844, much to Geary's pleasure. His buildings, including this little lodge, are still standing.

Mausoleum, Kensal Green Cemetery, North Kensington
Kensal Green Cemetery was opened in 1833 as the vanguard of the great Victorian cemeteries laid out around London. A competition held for the design of the cemetery buildings was won by Henry Kendall, one of the founders of the Royal Institute of British Architects, who in 1832 published *Sketches of the Approved Designs of a Chapel and Gateway Entrances*, intended to be erected at Kensal Green, in a robust Gothic. The word 'approved' was seen as a strong condemnation of the banker Sir John Dean Paul, Chairman of the General Cemetery Co., whose personal preference for the Greek style had led him to appoint the architect John Griffith of Finsbury in place of Kendall. Griffith landscaped the grounds with inspiration drawn from Nash's Regent's Park, using a central circle and dividing the rest into quadrants, one being reserved for Jews, Turks, Infidels and Heretics. Many famous names are buried here: Thackeray, Trollope, Terence Rattigan, the gardener J. C. Loudon, Blondin, Wilkie Collins, Rev. Sydney Smith and lesser names such as Captain Erle Elton, killed on 11 December 1899 at Magersfontein during the Boer War, whose tomb this is.

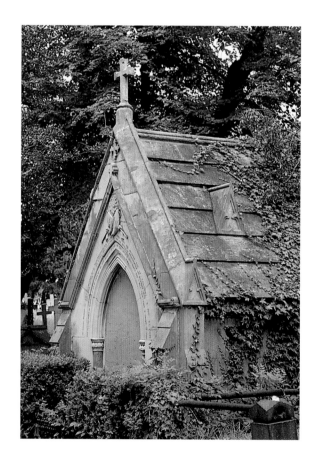

Victoria Gate Lodge, Hyde Park
Decimus Burton designed a lodge
for this site, but the end result
was built to the drawings of William
Crane in 1838. It is now occupied by
the assistant manager of Hyde Park
Gardens. These tiny gravestones
mark the site of a pet cemetery,
inaugurated by the Duke of
Cambridge in 1881. The first dog
to be buried here was Cherry,
belonging to the children of Mrs
Barnard Lewis of Cambridge
Square, followed by Prince, the
Duchess of Cambridge's dog.
It was full by 1903, and now only
dogs with family vaults can be
buried here. The inscriptions are
alternately heartrending and
baffling: 'Could love have
saved/Thou hadst not died'; 'Fritz,
a martyr.'

Waterlow Park Lodge, Waterlow Park, Highgate

Waterlow Park was given to the London County Council in 1889 by Sir Sidney Waterlow. Lauderdale, the main house in the park, was named after the Duke of Lauderdale, who lived here before dying at Tunbridge Wells in 1682, 'worn out by debaucheries'. Nell Gwynne also lived here. This lodge in Swain's Lane, a gentrification of Swine's Lane, was built opposite a demolished row of cottages in which lived a cow-keeper named John Rolls. His great-grandson founded the motor car company. The house has just been painstakingly restored.

Prince of Wales Gate Lodge, South Carriage Drive, Hyde Park, *below*
Decimus Burton's first lodge for Hyde Park was built in 1825, the start of a long and distinguished career. This one was designed by Burton for John Elger, who built the gate and lodges. The West Lodge was built in 1846, the East Lodge in 1851 as a police station for the Great Exhibition.

Kensington Palace Gardens
Better known to Londoners as 'Millionaire's Row', this expensive piece of real estate was built on the site of the old kitchen gardens of Kensington Palace – hence its official name of Kensington Palace Gardens – with the intention of attracting 'a superior class of tenants'. A frenzy of stucco peaks, it is as if one had stumbled into a Brobdingnagian cake-icing factory. It was developed by John Blashfield, a manufacturer of tesselated pavements. Like an alarming number of other Victorian developers, his scheme bankrupted him and he went down for over £40,000 in 1847.

North Gate Lodge was built in 1845 at a cost of £1,200 by the architects T. H. Wyatt and D. Brandon, in an Italianate style which was lauded for its correctness by the *Illustrated London News* the following year.

Alexandra Gate Lodge, Hyde Park

No building in the Royal Parks can be sold or leased. They can, however, be let, and the Alexandra Gate Lodge is let to a gardener from one of the firms which is subcontracted by the Royal Parks Agency to maintain the park.

This is one of the park's later lodges. Originally there was a wicket gate at this spot for pedestrians, but the gate was widened for carriages to visit the 1862 exhibition. The lodge, probably designed by C.J. Richardson, was added in 1868 and named after the then Princess of Wales.

Ivy Cottage, Kensington Palace, *above left*
Nottingham Cottage, Kensington Palace,
below left
Wren House, Kensington Palace, *right*

When William and Mary came jointly to the throne in 1688, the royal palace was in Whitehall. Buckingham Palace had not yet been built. Whitehall then was urban, teeming, smoky and filthy, not the elegant, austere boulevard we see today. King William suffered from asthma, and preferred the rural tranquillity and clear air of the great palace at Hampton Court. His advisers pressed him to live closer to Whitehall, and Queen Mary discovered a country villa called Nottingham House, close to the Middlesex village of Kensington and just two miles from Whitehall. William and Mary bought the house from Sir Heneage Finch, Earl of Nottingham, for £18,000 in 1689. Sir Christopher Wren was instructed to turn it into Kensington Palace, modest by the general standard of palaces. Even the sublime Wren occasionally faltered. Work started in July 1689. That November it was dispassionately noted that 'the additional buildings to the King's house at Kensington, being newly covered with lead, fell down on a sudden, and hurt several people and killed some.'

Queen Victoria was born at Kensington Palace in 1819. The old Nottingham House is remembered in the name of one of these comfortable cottages. The unremarkable Wren Cottage is so-called because it is said that Sir Christopher lived here on site during the building of the Palace. Mr. Mole, maintenance manager of Kensington Palace and its curtilage buildings, has lived in Ivy Cottage for 21 years. Despite being clearly named on the porch, it is always and only known as The Foreman's Cottage.

Central Pavilion, Coram's Fields, Bloomsbury
There are nine acres of central London where no adult may enter unless accompanied by a child. This is Coram's Fields, the site of the old Foundling Hospital, set up by the childless seafarer Captain Thomas Coram in 1739.

Hogarth's painting of Thomas Coram shows a robust, cheery, hearty fellow in late middle age, but by all accounts he was a hard man, untypically moved to pity by the not uncommon sight of babies discarded in London streets. Petitioning, pleading, campaigning, cajoling, persuading, bullying, Coram put an astonishing amount of hard work into founding the hospital. Within three years he was ousted by its committee.

Within a stone pier was a revolving niche for the 'All-Comer's Basket' hung up at the gate, a chaotic admissions policy where mothers could deposit their unwanted babies and ring the bell for the porter, a kind of baby bank. The first day the plan was introduced, 117 babies were left; 425 in the first month. The system was ended in 1769.

The original Hospital and its ancillary buildings were designed by Theodore Jacobsen on a 56-acre site. Coram was grateful for the support of London artists led by Hogarth, who instituted an annual gathering of artists and architects at the Hospital which led to the foundation of the Royal Academy. The site was sold in 1926 for development, but 9 acres were saved by Viscount Rothermere. The inscription to Coram in the southern arcade of the Hospital chapel reads: 'A man eminent in that most eminent virtue, the love of mankind.' The Foundling Hospital is now the Thomas Coram Foundation for Children.

The cartouche, *left*, is joined by railings, to flanking lodges, *right*.

The Hermitage, Church Road, Hanwell

The cottage ornée is not an uncommon survival in Britain, but it is certainly remarkable in London. They began to appear towards the end of the eighteenth century, an affected vernacular calling for a return to the simpler things in life. Arcadian dreams of shepherds and shepherdesses frolicking in a perpetual spring have always exerted a powerful hold on the leisured classes, the most notorious example being Marie-Antoinette playing out rural scenes at her sham dairy at Le Hameau in Versailles. This strange survival has a grim tale attached: it was built in 1809 by Mr Glasse, the rector of Hanwell and treasurer of a charity called the Hobbayne Trust, who hanged himself one night after leaving the entire funds of the trust in a hansom cab. The cab driver returned with the money to find the parson had acted too precipitately.

Wilfred Mark Webb, founder of the Selborne Society for the appreciation of the great Hampshire naturalist Gilbert White, bought the Hermitage in 1913, added 3 acres of land and built a lake. The present owner bought the house thirty years ago after it had languished on the market unsold for over a year.

William Hickey's Almshouses, Sheen Road, Richmond

Richmond has always been a favoured resort of royalty and nobility, and where wealth congregates so do attendants, who eventually retire and have to be pensioned off. This may explain the sudden proliferation of almshouses in this part of the borough, with the Richmond Church Estate Almshouses, the Houblon Almshouses and the Wlliam Hickey Almshouses almost buttress to buttress along the Sheen road. Hickey's almshouses were designed and built by Lewis Vulliamy in 1832–5, an early essay by one of our great Victorian Gothic church architects. Here his work is hesitant and unsure, as if this were an early practice piece before going on to pointed success.

The Coach House, Fitzgerald Avenue, Barnes

So much of London mushroomed in the second half of the nineteenth century that it is hard to differentiate rows of houses that are twenty miles apart. The homely monotony of the London terrace is very occasionally disrupted by rogue architecture like this. This was a coach-house for the now demolished Gladesmuir, built by Jonadab Hanks of Stamford Brook. Never mind that the datestone reads 1696; it's a lie. 'This Is My House The House Of Prayer' thunders the Latin inscription, a strange sentiment for a stable, but salvaged, like much of the rest of this bizarre little construction kit, from long-forgotten buildings. Thus it was said that this little house originated as the Marylebone School for Girls by Sir Christopher Wren, and was reconstructed here by Jonadab. There is no proof of this, but local legend is seldom completely without foundation. The house looked even odder before the First World War when it had four immense Elizabethan chimneys at each corner, but these were taken down as it was feared that 'vibrations from Zeppelins' may have toppled them.

Dudley House, Clive Road, Dulwich

In 1882 Ralph Gardiner came to Dulwich College from Dudley in Worcestershire, to take up the post of Master Plasterer. There could be no better demonstration of his virtuosity than to show the trustees of the College an entire room that he had created in a house he had built. Dudley House is long and thin, cleverly designed to make the best use of a strip of land only 16 feet wide, and into this straitened slot he crammed a three-bedroomed house with garden and a living-room so elaborately plastered it's like entering a wedding cake. Gardiner was successful enough at Dulwich to enter into a little development on his own account; he laid out and built the houses in nearby Chalford Road.

Grosvenor Road, Pimlico
Hidden behind the towering blocks of Powell &
Moya's pioneering post-war public housing at
Churchill Gardens are the wrought-iron
verandahs and prettily curved paths of this
former riverside terrace, a late Regency haven
of human-scale architecture buttressed by a
rectory at one end and the King William IV pub
at the other. Churchill Gardens has received
architectural plaudits from the start; other,
inferior copies have given the genre its poor
reputation. But faced with the soulless,
monumental anonymity of the mass-designed
council flat, however brilliantly conceived, who
would not prefer the hidden promise implicit in
this intriguing, beckoning entrance? The
drawback is that the terrace is now separated
from the river front by Grosvenor Road, better
known as the Embankment and one of the
busiest roads in London.

Douglas Road, Islington

It comes as a surprise to discover among the quiet, civilized Georgian understatement of Canonbury terraces this refugee from De Stijl, a house surely more at home in Dessau or Utrecht than in conventional, neophobic London. At first glance it could have been built at any time in the twentieth century; closer inspection reveals its newness, built by the architectural group Future Systems for a private client in 1994. Privacy and glass houses don't often go together; this manages both successfully. The constant amazement for Londoners is how the builders ever managed to get planning permission, especially in a conservation area. Apparently the planning officers were enthusiastic about the design, requesting only that the trees on the site be kept – which allows the path to sweep up to the entrance in unconscious imitation of the Regency elegance of the Grosvenor Road terrace on the opposite page.

Albert Mews, Kensington

Thomas Pennant, the eighteenth-century Welsh travel writer, noted 'On the North side of Charing-cross stand the royal stables, called from the original use of the building on their site, the mews: having been used for keeping the king's falcons, at least from the time of Richard II.'

The mews of London were built as the stables and service wings of the grand town houses they backed on to, and the buildings were usually occupied by the coach and coachman. The source of the curious word 'mews' comes from falconry, as Pennant indicated: a mew was a cage for moulting birds of prey, mew meaning to moult or to change, from the same root as mutate. They all derived their name from the original royal mews.

London mews have themselves now largely mutated into bijou houses, but Albert Mews, built in 1865 by Charles Aldin, still retains more of its original character than most. Access to the rooms above would have been by external staircase. 'Albert' is the second most common street name in the capital, the first of course being Victoria.

Canal Bridge Entrance, Lisson Grove, St John's Wood

When is a tunnel not a tunnel? When it passes under a house, a road and a small garden according to the builders of the Regents Canal, a mere trifle before a short open stretch and it disappears into the 272 yards of the Maida Hill Tunnel. The canal is a good 60 feet below ground level here, a very deep cut, and this has the potential to be the grandest entrance on the Canal. It is quite grand, but not quite grand enough. The building swallowing the boat looks ambitious but uneducated; some inspiration from the Italian Mannerists such as Count Orsini at Bomarzo would have been far more exciting than this strangled Protestant Palladianism. Yet compared to the front, the back is a triumph. High up above on Lisson Grove, the street façade of the house is a singular disappointment, an easily overlooked single-storey brick shed with a pitiful pediment above the cheap front door. It is now an office for an anonymous company, squeezed into a triangular shape out of necessity rather than through any sense of adventure.

Junction Cottage, Blomfield Road, Little Venice

On the Paddington arm of the Grand Union Canal hard by the Warwick Avenue bridge is this canal worker's cottage currently being refurbished by the Waterways Board, as the property prices in Little Venice have soared.

Toll House, Spaniard's Inn, Hampstead, *left*

The Spaniards is one of London's best-known pubs, said to have been built in 1585 as the Spanish Ambassador's residence. However, the name comes from two Spanish brothers who ran the inn here at the beginning of the seventeenth century. The staff here are provided with handy place mats which outline the history of the inn, including tales of the notorious highwayman Dick Turpin whose father was once the landlord of the house, and its inevitable mention in Dickens's *Pickwick Papers*. Opposite the pub, forming a well-known chicane on the Hampstead Lane, is this toll gate at the entrance to the Bishop of London's estates, on the site of a lodge erected for the keeper of Park Gate.

Thatchedhouse Lodge, Richmond Park,
left and *below left*

Richmond Park has 2,358 acres, big by
any British standards, vast for any City
park. This is because London has
swallowed it; formerly in Surrey, it was
protected as a royal hunting park, with a
10-mile perimeter wall. Thatchedhouse
Lodge is a large thatched house, which
was probably built around 1727 for the
Prime Minister, Sir Robert Walpole. In a
very English reversal of the status quo,
where a lodge prefigures the main
house, Thatchedhouse Lodge has in its
garden the actual Thatched House, an
enchanting little summer-house with a
thatched roof and a balcony overlooking
the valley. The creator of this rural
delight is not known; Pevsner thought it
could be by William Kent, but there is no
proof other than records of Kent working
on other projects for Walpole at the time.
Sir John Soane redesigned the dining-
room in 1798, which led to him being
credited with the whole house, which
had been built 25 years before his birth.

Buckhill Lodge, Kensington Gardens
One of those delightful houses with gables where there was never need of gables,' as E. Nesbit wrote. The gable is probably the first architectural feature a lay person notices – few houses are called The Columns or The Pediments. The steeper the pitch of the roof, the more exuberant the gables can be, in some cases carried to excess, as we see here. Buckhill Lodge, originally occupied by the foreman of Kensington Gardens, was built in 1852 and altered in 1888. The elegant carving of the bargeboards can be seen in the close-up of the porch.

Broad Walk Refreshment Lodge, Regent's Park
Bargeboarding conveys a rustic, rural, forested life, especially when carried to vertical extremes. This little kiosk has only one floor. It may look like a weather house, but it has been dispensing refreshments to strollers in Regent's Park since 1850.

**Spinning Wheel Thatched Lodge,
South Street, Bromley**
Although this may look lovely, use of a
wide-angle lens would have revealed the
ghastly road-house-style Family Pubbe
that lurks behind this cute cottage ornée.
This is where the manager lives.

Round House, Woodside Park, Wood Green

'There were dozens of these bizarre little toys in the London countryside, but hardly any have survived,' lamented Sir John Summerson. Of the few that have, not many are as individualistic as this substantial round house in north London. It was built in 1822 as one of twin lodges to the now-vanished Chitts Hill Manor, still standing in the early twentieth century before the entire area was carpeted with terraced housing.

Erected towards the end of the fashion for cottages ornées, the design was copied from John Plaw's influential pattern book *Sketches for Country Houses, Villas and Rural Dwellings*, published in 1800. Plaw was the architect of Belle Isle in Windermere, the only circular stately home in Britain, and was a master of the genre. The building is a remarkable survival for a rural building on an urban main road, and has suffered love and neglect in equal measure. Starting life as a lodge, it became an ornamental dairy, after which it was used as a children's play house; then it was derelict for years and now it is fully restored and occupied. The fishscale tiled roof has unfortunately replaced the original thatch.

Cumberland Gate Lodge, Hyde Park

A brutally heavy entablature – perhaps extended to contain the clock – overbalances this nearly classical composition. All the elements are present and correct, but they are lined up and sized in some confusion. This is monumentality on a less-than-human scale, and the inclusion of unsightly uPVC windows either side of the Doric columns is the camel's nose under the tent. Another early work by Decimus Burton, it was taken down in 1851 to make way for the repositioning of Marble Arch, then as a public convenience on Park Lane in 1857. Over a century later in 1961 it was moved again to Cumberland Gate, and now serves as a dwelling for the assistant manager of St James's Park.

Lodge, Park Square West, Regent's Park

These tiny Greek lodges – there are four of them – were built by John Nash between 1823–5, flanking the triumphal entry to Regent's Park from Park Crescent and Portland Place, at the top of Regent Street. Calmly settled alongside the frenetic Marylebone Road, they must be the most visible lodges in London, always immaculately maintained and just large enough for an intimate picnic.

Lodge, Hyde Park Corner

In 1822 Decimus Burton built this Greek Doric lodge, now used by the Friends of Hyde Park. Burton was just 25 when he secured this high-profile commission, but he was already an experienced architect, having designed The Holme in Regent's Park for his father when he was just eighteen. The turret clock, by Thwaites & Reeds, was added in 1844. Burton's screen of fluted Ionic columns, with a frieze by John Henning copied directly from the Parthenon, was erected in 1827 on the adjoining Apsley Gate, named for the Duke of Wellington's house at the other end, and was intended to be adorned with statues.

Sham Chapel, Sidcup

The traffic and trading estates of south-east London conceal a palimpsest of parkland and rustic charm. Occasionally, a relic of this vanished bucolic age breaks through the fabric of our concrete era to puzzle, if not startle, the passer-by. In the eighteenth century it was the norm rather than the exception to adorn one's country estate with buildings for the sake of themselves; buildings for pleasure before purpose, buildings which we in a less enlightened age called follies. These structures took on many forms, and not the least familiar was the sham chapel, or artificial church. This secular wonder even took different forms, sometimes artfully ruined, sometimes an estate dwelling, sometimes simply an eye-catcher. Crushed between a roundabout and a timber yard is this doughty survivor from Georgian times, a prettily Gothicized sham chapel, converted from a cottage in 1770 to serve as an eye-catcher from Danson Park and still capable of fooling the neighbours.

The Lodge, Aberdeen Park, Highbury

About the only mark this quiet and private estate has made on history is when the great red church at its heart was the subject of a post-war Betjeman poem.

Aberdeen Park was developed from 1853, and named after the 4th Earl of Aberdeen, the then Prime Minister. The land was owned by George Morrice, and his brother the Rev. W. D. Morrice built the 'great Victorian church, tall, unbroken and bright' of St Saviour's to seat 568 worshippers in 1866.

In 1806 a Captain Agnew lived in a house 'with offices and pleasure grounds' on the site of Aberdeen Park. In 1997 the estate agents who were selling the lodge, carefully described as a 'coach house,' assumed it dated back to that time. Sadly for these royal and ancient stories the lodge was actually built sometime between 1870 and 1890. It does not appear on an extremely detailed 1869 map, but by 1892 it is shown at the end of Aberdeen Park Road, at the entrance to the estate.

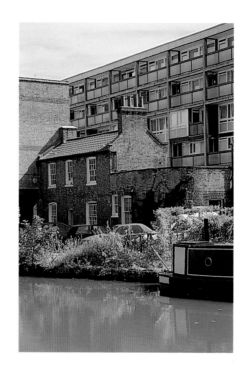

Lock House, City Road, Islington

A boat navigating its way along the Grand Union towards the Thames emerges from the 960-yard-long Islington Tunnel and cruises along a shaded stretch of canal past an extraordinary Nash terrace of castellated stucco backings on Noel Road, well screened by the residents' competitive tree culture. Continuing under Frog Hall Bridge, which carries Danbury Street over the canal, it approaches the City Road lock and weir, just before the City Road basin. Here the redundant lock-keeper's cottage is dwarfed by public housing and warehouses revamped to suit fashionable design studios.

Paynes Wharf, fronting Borthwick Street, Deptford

A row of six mighty arches have dwarfed this overseer's little white office on the edge of the Upper Watergate Stairs in Deptford since 1860. They fronted the boiler works of John Penn & Sons, a major nineteenth-century marine engineering company. The company ceased trading in 1913 and the arches have stood here in remembrance ever since.

To the right of the stairs is Convoys Wharf, formerly the Old Royal Naval Dockyard, and now the largest working wharf in London. Despite the gentrification of East London, despite the closure of the mighty docks on the Isle of Dogs, despite the redevelopment of Canary Wharf, despite all this London remains Britain's busiest port.

Wharfinger Cottage and Currency Exchange House, Tower of London
The wharf at the Tower of London was the work of Adam de Lamburn for Henry III, 'Henry the Builder' in 1240, and was regarded as one of the wonders of his reign. Shortly after completion on St George's Night 1240 the wall collapsed, and had to be rebuilt. It collapsed again on the same night the following year. Nevertheless Henry completed the wharf the following year, and there it has remained ever since.

Wharfinger Cottage was originally built in the seventeenth century as the residence of the Controller of Tower Wharf. This nineteenth-century half-timbered replacement, described as 'preposterously domesticated' by Pevsner, may well have been by the major Victorian architect Anthony Salvin as there are similarities between this and the architect's own house at Fernhurst in Sussex. Certainly the adjacent tall, grim Tower Engine House of 1863, now a currency exchange shop for tourists, was by him.

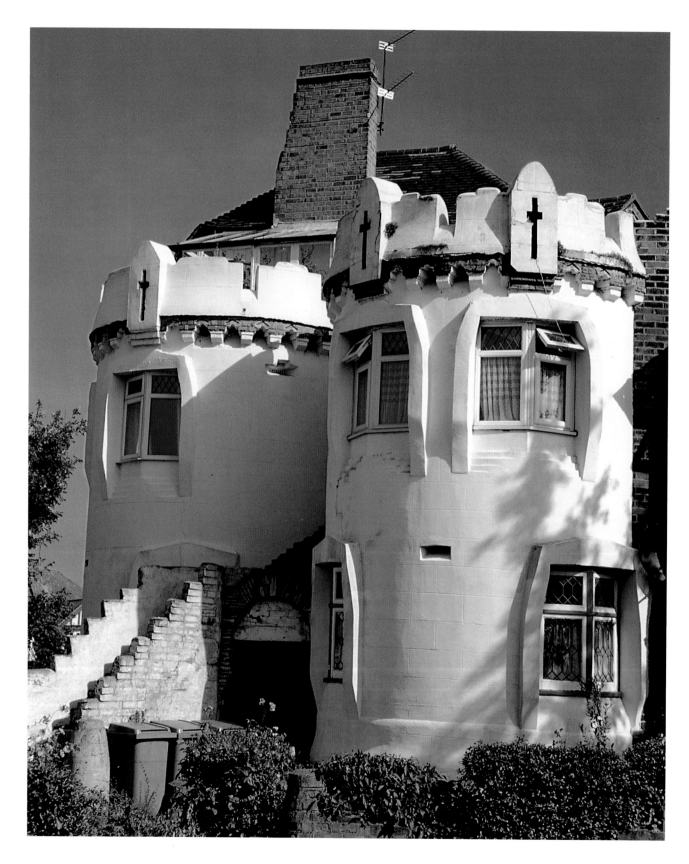

Castle Houses, Buck Lane, Kingsbury

Belfast-born Ernest Trobridge came to London on a mission, a mission which even today is hard to understand. The easy explanation is that he had a romantic view of Olde England, a view of thatched cottages and clapboarded houses, castles and smoke curling up from barley-sugar chimneys, but he restricted himself to what he could build. Trobridge worked in a field now known faintly contemptuously as 'design and build'. In Trobridge's case, he was both designer and builder, and it is clear which role he preferred. After success with an early pre-fab at the 1920 Ideal Home Exhibition, he was encouraged to begin speculative building on 10 acres of the sweeping open hills of north-west London, on the borders of burgeoning Metroland. In 1934 his favoured style was Tudor, not the bypass Tudor of well-deserved scorn and derision, but an impressively authentic facsimile of the period with herringbone brickwork. A year later he had travelled back stylistically eight hundred years to Rochester Castle, and produced these whited wonders on top of Wakeman's Hill. Buck, Stag and Slough Lanes in Kingsbridge all have examples of his eclectic art.

Lodge, Fulham Palace

The taste for the picturesque came late to the Church, but when it arrived it was embraced with fervour. Fulham Palace is one of the least known of London's major buildings – many Londoners would mistake a picture of it for Hampton Court. Somehow its nineteenth-century lodge suffers from the same anonymity.

Sir William Powell Almshouses, Fulham

In 1680 Sir William Powell endowed these almshouses close by All Saints, the parish church of the then village of Fulham. They were rebuilt in a rather romantic style in 1869 by J. P. Seddon, in an L-shape with a bell-tower at the entrance. Figures of Faith, Hope and Charity stand in deep niches, with the inscription 'God's Providence, Our Inheritance.'

**Curator's house,
Johnson Museum, Gough Square**

It seems only fair that the alleyway to the side of Dr Samuel Johnson's house, where the great lexicographer compiled his monumental *Dictionary of the English Language*, should be named after him, but it isn't: Johnson's Court is named after an otherwise forgotten tailor, not Samuel. In amends, Johnson's beloved cat Hodge is commemorated by a statue in Gough Square, one of only two statues in London to commemorate specific cats. This curious twin-doored little cottage houses the curator of the Johnson Museum, one of London's many *recherché* delights.

St Andrew's Church Lodge, Shoe Lane, Holborn

Before the Victorian Society re-educated us all in the merits of that much derided period of architecture, S. S. Teulon more than any other architect epitomized the style and spirit of what we used to be allowed to call Victorian monstrosities. Even allowing for his apologists, Teulon produced much of the high Victorian work most hated by following generations: a generous use of diapering, lavish with lucarnes, topped out with turrets. His greatest critic was the architectural historian Sir Nikolaus Pevsner who seldom missed an opportunity in his *Buildings of England* series to berate Teulon's fecund diversity – but even he is complimentary about this perky little lodge, built some time between 1868 and 1871: an 'endearing little lodge with a big central chimneystack'.

The Russian House, The Vale, Chelsea

The Russian House is a twentieth-century addition to The Vale. In 1836 there were only four houses in the road, which ran from the King's Road to a Mr McGuire's deer-park. This was a grandiose title for a small field which held a smaller herd, but here they lived, in the middle of Chelsea, until creeping urbanization forced McGuire to consolidate his investment, sell the beasts and replace them with cement replicas. The park and the herd, real and cast, have long gone. The Russian House's black clapboarded first floor, with a Venetian window facing on to the street, is unique in London but commonplace in Russia where this architectural style is known as an 'izba', or Cossack peasant's hut. The building served as the Russian Pavilion at a turn-of-the-century exhibition, was purchased and re-erected here on a prime site commanding an uninterrupted view down Mallord Street.

**Pirates' Castle,
Oval Road, Camden**
England is not a country saturated in colour; muted greens and greys are favoured over the blatant scarlets, ochres and azures of the Mediterranean, except when it comes to canal boats. They drift through the countryside like floating harlequins, a testimony, one might think, to the artistry and creativity of the boaters. Not so. The narrow boats were generally decorated by dock painters, apprenticed professionals who painted and refurbished boats in their yards. The traditional good fortune motifs of castles and roses which ornament so many boats were sometimes painted by the owners, but the decorative shapes of diamonds, cubes, lozenges, circles and squares were the preserve of the dock painters. The castellations seen above the bridge are from the Pirates' Castle – a youth club designed by R. Seifert & Partners and built in 1977 to look like a little fortress.

Tower Bridge, City of London

Here's a splendid example of Victorian assertiveness and confidence married to typical English sentimentality. Tower Bridge is one of the great London icons, an image recognized around the world, and now welcomes visitors by the thousand. Looking almost as old as its close neighbour the Tower of London, Tower Bridge is none the less a fraud. Building began in July 1886, and it was completed in July 1894. It is a state of the art (for its time) steel-framed buiding, the last word in bascule bridges, and its ecclesiastical elegance comes from stone cladding, the model for thousands of suburban eyesores in the 1980s. Perched at the very top of this mighty tower was the bridge-master's residence, 'a comfortable and commodious apartment' with fine views of London.

Albany, Piccadilly

Flanked by discreetly expensive shops is the entrance to Albany, where once stood the mansion of the Duke of York & Albany, who sold it to a speculator in 1808 with the proviso that 'no trade or profession' was to be carried on, as that would interfere with the gentility of the place. The clause was maintained, and these gentlemen's chambers in this most private heart of London remain unsullied by commercialism. Neither whistling nor running are allowed. The rooms were (and are) let to young and not so young men about town, and from the start it was an aspirational address; so much so that by the 1830s a 'Bachelor of Albany' was a prince among such society. Charles Dickens dismissed its pretensions in a phrase: 'a very convenient thoroughfare for those who have the audacity to use it,' and the same holds true today.

The Old Curiosity Shop, Portsmouth Street, Holborn

A one-bay, two-storey, seventeenth-century shop with overhanging upper storey and a turnerized roof (sprayed with asphalt), conspicuously picturesque but obliterated by the economic conformity of the buildings towering around it. In Dickens's eponymous bestseller, Little Nell and her anonymous grandfather fled the shop, leaving it in the hands of the evil dwarf Quilp, and 'the old house was a patch of darkness among its gaily lit neighbours'. Today the roles are reversed: Portsmouth Street is one of the bleakest, most anonymous byways in central London. Incidentally Dickens wrote that the Old Curiosity Shop was torn down after Little Nell's death. But that was fiction, and this is fact.

**Francis Walters Funeral Directors,
Commercial Road, Limehouse**

This tiny undertakers' office on the Commercial
Road opened in 1902, but when English
Heritage came round in 1992 they dated parts
of it back to the seventeenth century.
Underneath the plasticky 1960s fascia they
discovered the faded lettering for Ward &
Walters, Builders and Funeral Directors, and
indeed when Mr Wagstaff the present manager
came to the firm in 1967, coffins were still
being made on the premises in the old builders'
yard 'out the back', where their chapel of rest
now stands. Once the old 'new' fascia had been
removed, the front was refurbished to
its dignified turn-of-the-century splendour.

Dog House, Ranger's Lodge, Wimbledon

Nothing lasts for ever in this transient world, and many things are not meant to, like these two oddities. The structure below is officially classed as a 'Building – Relocatable', and in case one is unsure of its purpose a large sign is attached to it, spelling it out.

The Bromptons, South Kensington

All is not what it seems. When this magnificent 'building' is finally pulled down, it will reveal a pastiche of a pastiche, a twenty-first-century reworking of a mid-nineteenth-century re-creation of a Tudor college or cloister. It was built as a hospital for consumptives in 1844–6 by the architect F. J. Francis, who went on to build a couple of churches in south London before quietly vanishing into Victorian obscurity. But he clearly had fun here; there was a lot of work and a lot of building to do, and to those Londoners who have been accustomed for years to a blackened mass of Victorian brickwork cluttering up the Fulham Road just as it begins to get interesting, its renovation and refurbishment as a block of luxury flats will be welcomed.

Eyecatcher Arch, *right*, and Lodges, *below*, Syon House, Brentford
The great changes at Syon were wrought during the reign of Sir Hugh Smithson, the 1st Duke of Northumberland. Lancelot Brown was paid £1,956 for landscaping the grounds, and the fashionable Adam brothers were employed to ornament the perimeter of the estate with these lodges and eye-catcher arches. One of the finest sights at Syon is the Great Conservatory, built by Charles Fowler for the 3rd Duke in 1820–7, long before Paxton made huge cast-iron glasshouses famous.

The Lion Gate, Syon House, Brentford
In 1773 Horace Walpole wrote to the Rev. William Mason about '...a magnificent gateway and screen for the Duke of Northumberland at Syon, which I see erecting every time I pass. It is all lace and embroidery, and as croquant [a form of decoration in Gothic archirecture] as his frames for tables; consequently most improper to be exposed in the high road to Brentford. From Kent's mahogany we are dwindled to Adam's filigree. Grandeur and simplicity are not yet a fashion.'

Old Isleworth Boathouse, Syon Park

Hugh Percy Smithson, the 1st Duke of Northumberland, favoured the Gothick style of architecture, and strewed his estate at Alnwick with fabulous towers, sham castles and eye-catchers. His heir, the 2nd Duke, preferred his estate at Syon House in Middlesex, and a more controlled, academic architecture. This epitome of Georgian elegance on the river started life as a boathouse – the Thames was formerly wider than it is today – built by the distinguished architect Robert Mylne. He was seventy when he designed this hyperborean Ionic temple for the 2nd Duke, but he had erupted on to the London scene as a young man of 27 when he had won the competition to design the new Blackfriars Bridge, against illustrious opposition. Mylne's architectural pedigree rivalled the lineage of the Emperor of Japan; he was the seventh recorded generation of his family to practise. This is perhaps best reflected in his estimate for the building of the bridge; it was costed at £153,003. Mylne bought the project in on time and at a final cost of £152,840.

The tide still comes in far enough for the boathouse to be utilitarian as well as beautiful, but this is no longer a concern since it was converted into a refined private house in the 1950s by the architects Pinkney & Gott, who added the flanking wings to Mylne's original rotunda.

> There Sion lifts her venerable pile,
> Where hospitality still wears a smile;
> Where taste and elegance and grandeur shine,
> And every virtue decks brave Piercy's line!
> See vary'd vessels here with flags advance,
> And o'er the waves in mazy figures dance;
> Pass and repass, and trim the swelling sail,
> And sport and wanton in the breezy gale.

Acknowledgments

First and foremost I would like to thank Gwyn Headley for his wonderful knowledge of London and love of architecture, as well as his scholarly research and not least, his marvellous and engaging company while we searched the city. I would particularly like to thank Ray Watkins for working with such meticulous care and talent on the layout, typography and design of the book. Hannah Christopherson for her patience, organizing, and planning the many excursions. Michael Dover for publishing it, and Anthony Lambert for his editing.

Index of buildings

First published in Great Britain in 1999
by Weidenfeld & Nicolson

Photographs copyright © Snowdon 1999
Text copyright © Gwyn Headley 1999
The moral right of Snowdon and Gwyn Headley to be identified as the authors of this work has been asserted in accordance
with the Copyright, Designs and Patents Act of 1988
Design and layout copyright © Weidenfeld & Nicolson, 1999

A CIP catalogue record for this book is available from the British Library
ISBN 0 297 82490 2

Designed by Price Watkins
Edited by Anthony J. Lambert
Printed and Bound in Italy
Set in Bauer Bodoni and Din

Weidenfeld & Nicolson
The Orion Publishing Group Ltd
5 Upper St Martin's Lane
London WC2H 9EA

Many people have generously spared their time to help with the research for this book, and Gwyn Headley would particularly like to thank: Phil Ashford, Des Barber, Hilary Bradt, Maisie Brown, Mike Brown, John Cloaken, Elizabeth Cory, John Davison, Nicolette Duckham, Mark Dykes, Oliver Everett, Tim Everson, Vernon Gibberd, Lesley Gillilan, Iain Gray, Jan Gold, Stephen Gould, Peter Hodge, Guy Holborn, Elizabeth Anne Jarrett, Esther Kirland, Richard Lines, Dave Loughton, David Macdonald, David March, Gordon Matthewman, Hugh McKnight, Wim Meulenkamp, Eric Montague, Joan Plachta Nash, Dr. Nicholas Newton, Kate Nichol, PS David Noall, Peter Osgood, PC Dick Paterson, Anthony Powell, Dr Anne Richards, Phil 'The Eel' Sanders, Shirley Seaton, Yvonne Seeley, Jenny Sheridan, Jan Sutherland, Mr Waghorn, Eileen Watling, Valerie Wenham, Margaret Willes, Kate Williamson